BIG BOOK OF
SCROLL SAW
WOODWORKING

More Than 60 Projects and Techniques for Fretwork, Intarsia & Other Scroll Saw Crafts

BIG BOOK OF
SCROLL SAW
WOODWORKING

More Than 60 Projects and Techniques for Fretwork, Intarsia & Other Scroll Saw Crafts

from the editors of *Scroll Saw Woodworking & Crafts Magazine*

From Photo to Pattern
Custom Intarsia Designs
By Kathy Wise, page 115

FOX CHAPEL
PUBLISHING

© 2009 by Fox Chapel Publishing Company, Inc.

Big Book of Scroll Saw Woodworking is an original work, first published in 2009 by Fox Chapel Publishing Company, Inc. The patterns contained herein are copyrighted by the authors. Readers may make copies of these patterns for personal use. The patterns themselves, however, are not to be duplicated for resale or distribution under any circumstances. Any such copying is a violation of copyright law.

ISBN 978-1-56523-426-0

Publisher's Cataloging-in-Publication Data

    Big book of scroll saw woodworking : more than 60 projects and

    techniques for fretwork, intarsia & other scroll saw crafts / by the

    editors of Scroll saw woodworking & crafts. -- 1st ed. -- East

    Petersburg, PA : Fox Chapel Publishing, c2009

       p. ; cm.

       (The best of Scroll saw woodworking & crafts)

       ISBN: 978-1-56523-426-0

       Includes index.

       1. Jig saws-- Patterns. 2. Woodwork--Patterns. I. Title.

    II. Series. III. Title: Scroll saw woodworking & crafts.

TT199.7 .B54 2009
745.51/3--dc22   2009

To learn more about the other great books from Fox Chapel Publishing, or to find a retailer near you, call toll-free 800-457-9112 or visit us at *www.FoxChapelPublishing.com*.

Note to Authors: We are always looking for talented authors to write new books in our area of woodworking, design, and related crafts. Please send a brief letter describing your idea to Acquisition Editor, 1970 Broad Street, East Petersburg, PA 17520.

Printed in Indonesia
First printing
Second printing
Third printing

Table of Contents

What You Can Make

Beginning Patterns, page 18

Puzzles and Toys, page 26

Inlay and Relief, page 42

Personalizing, page 54

Baskets and Boxes, page 66

Compound Cutting, page 96

Intarsia and Segmentation, page 106

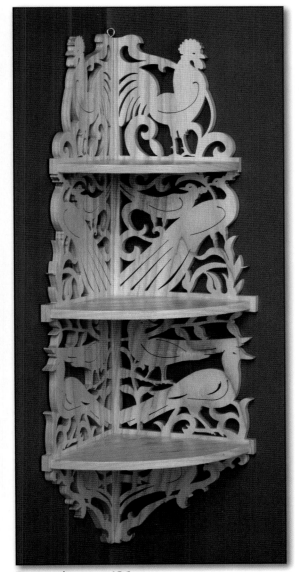

Fretwork, page 136

Portraits, page 156

Materials Other Than Wood, page 172

Introduction

Your scroll saw can do so many things, we needed a big book to hold them all! *Scroll Saw Woodworking & Crafts* magazine is proud to present this collection of some of our best projects for scrollers just starting out and for those who have experience. On the following pages, you'll find not only patterns from many of our contributors, but also tips, techniques, stories, and, hopefully, inspiration for trying the projects featured here and your own creations.

This book is broken down by category so that you can easily find the type of project you'd like to try—from boxes and clocks to intarsia and fretwork. Whether you are a beginning scroller looking to sample some of the different types of things you can do with a scroll saw or an experienced scroller looking to try other areas of scrolling, this book provides a great reference for your next projects and many projects to come. So jump on in. What will your favorite scroll saw technique be?

Getting Started

If you're just starting out, the following tips and techniques can help you on your way to scroll saw success. Read through the information here before you actually begin at your saw.

Safety

Though the scroll saw is a relatively safe tool, take the time to make sure you're working safely. Check that your work area is clean, well-lit, well-ventilated, and uncluttered. A dust collector, mask, air cleaner, or a combination of these items can help protect your lungs from fine dust.

Check that you are dressed appropriately. Wear some type of safety goggles just in case a piece of wood should break free and fly toward your face and eyes. Remove any loose clothing or jewelry before you operate the saw.

Of course, don't work while you are tired, and always keep your hands and fingers a safe distance away from the blade.

It's a good idea to read through the instructions before you begin to make sure that you understand everything involved. Also, gather your tools at the beginning so everything is close at hand. The projects here list the general tools you'll need and often give other suggestions and options. Remember, however, the lists are simply guidelines, and you should always work with tools you feel comfortable using.

Selecting the Materials

Invest some time in selecting the appropriate material for your project, whether it's hardwood, plywood, or some other nonwood material. The material you choose will affect not only how the finished piece looks, but also how easy it is to cut, sand, and finish.

No matter what material you choose, be sure it is flat—not cupped or warped—and relatively free of defects, such as knots. Buy quartersawn wood when available because it is the most stable.

Hardwoods often create very beautiful finished projects although they can be a little harder to work with than plywood. Mixing different colors of hardwoods also can produce a striking effect. If you are relatively new to scrolling, high-quality Baltic birch plywood can be easier to use than hardwoods and takes stain well if you want to simulate color contrasts.

Also consider what the right thickness is for your particular project. Especially if you are a new scroller, do not

Hardwoods offer a variety of colors and grain patterns that can enhance your projects. Shown here from left to right are catalpa, red oak, cherry, birch, black walnut, white oak, mahogany, and American aromatic cedar.

cut material that is too thick or too thin. If the wood is too thick, you can be frustrated with blade breakage, burning of the material, and difficulty getting through the project. If the wood is too thin, it presents another set of problems, including not enough resistance to the blade, which makes it hard to turn and stay on the lines.

If you will be stack cutting your project, decide that as you select your material. $\frac{1}{16}$" and $\frac{1}{8}$" plywood are ideal for stacking.

Keep in mind that using a different thickness of wood than the one called for in the project can change the look of the finished piece. For example, using $\frac{3}{4}$" wood for a delicate ornament may not look as nice as the same pattern cut from $\frac{1}{8}$" wood.

Attaching Patterns

There are several different methods to attach or transfer patterns to a blank. It's really a matter of personal preference. Experiment with the various methods until you find the one that works best for you.

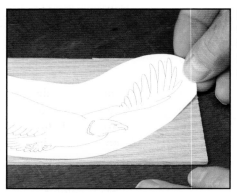

Smooth your pattern onto the stock from the inside out, removing any bubbles.

Temporary-bond spray adhesive: The most common method to attach a pattern to a blank is with temporary-bond spray adhesive. Rubber cement or glue sticks also work similarly. Start by photocopying the pattern. Place the pattern to be sprayed inside a cardboard box to contain any overspray. Then spray the adhesive on the back of the pattern (spray the paper pattern—not the wood), wait a few seconds, and press the pattern down onto the blank.

Applying the pattern over painters tape will aid in removal.

Clear packaging tape: This method is similar to the last method. Apply the spray adhesive as explained above. Then cover the pattern and work piece with strips of clear packaging tape. The tape holds the pattern down tightly. When you are finished, pull off the tape and the pattern usually comes off with it. Chemicals added to keep the tape from sticking to itself while on the roll will also help to lubricate your blade. Most scrollers recommend using clear packaging tape over the pattern when cutting thick or hard woods.

Large label: Copy the pattern onto a self-adhesive 8½" x 11" label. Then just peel the backing off, and attach it to the blank.

Painter's masking tape: Cover the blank with blue painter's tape. Then attach the pattern to the tape using the spray adhesive method. The blue painter's tape is formulated to be easy to remove and should not leave much of a residue on your blank. This tape is also coated with chemicals similar to those used in clear packaging tape that keep the tape from sticking to itself, so some scrollers coat their thick or hard woods with painters' tape as well.

Graphite or carbon transfer paper: Position the transfer paper on the blank with your pattern on top and use a few pieces of painter's tape to hold the pattern and transfer paper in place. Trace around the pattern with a red pen (so you know where you have traced). Use a white or light-colored transfer paper for darker woods. Carbon paper costs less, but is hard to remove and paint over. Graphite paper is more expensive, but is easier to remove after scrolling and is available in more colors. If you use carbon paper, a quick sanding with 220-grit sandpaper will remove most of the pattern lines.

Removing Patterns

If you attach a paper pattern to your work, you will need to remove it and any adhesive residue after cutting. Just like with pattern application, people prefer different methods. Try experimenting until you find the one you are most comfortable with.

Mineral spirits: Most of the time, the pattern will come off easily. A quick wipe of mineral spirits will remove any adhesive residue. You can also dampen the pattern with mineral spirits to aid in removal.

Adhesive remover: There are several adhesive removers on the market, with Goo Gone® being the most well known. Follow the manufacturer's instructions to remove the pattern.

Sanding: A light sanding with fine sandpaper (220-grit) will also remove the pattern and adhesive residue.

Blade-entry Holes

Blade-entry holes are the holes drilled for inside cuts. These are cuts that cannot be accessed from the scrap portion of your project. They allow you to insert the blade in an area that will be surrounded by the finished project—such as the inside of the letter "O." There are several things to take into account when making blade-entry holes.

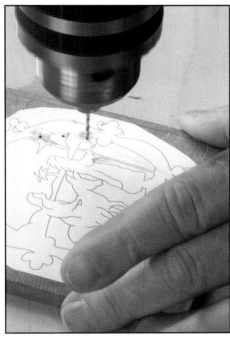

A drill press is recommended for perpendicular entry holes.

Location: Some patterns have blade-entry holes marked. If the pattern doesn't, use your best judgment. Place the holes near a line to be cut to prolong your blade life, but don't place the hole on a curving line (if possible). Also avoid putting the hole in a corner—inside corner cuts need to be sharp to look right.

Method: Drill the blade-entry hole perpendicular to the blank. Use a drill press if you have one. Drill through your blank into scrap wood to prevent tear out on the back side. Using a scrap wood backer will save you time sanding or scraping the back of your project.

Drill Bit Size: The diameter of your drill bit depends on the size of the area you are cutting and the size of your blade. If you have the space, use a larger bit—it will make it easier to thread your blade. For thin veining cuts, use the smallest-diameter bit your blade will fit through. Many scrollers sharpen the ends of their blades a little to allow them to pass through smaller entry holes.

Blade Tension

Most saws have a control mechanism to adjust the tension on the blade.

The tension should be completely removed before installing a blade. Clamp both ends of the blade into the blade holders and adjust the tension. A well-tensioned blade will produce a "C" pitch sound. For those who have trouble adjusting tension according to sound, try pushing the blade with your finger. It should flex no more than ⅛" forward, backward, or side to side.

A blade that does not have enough tension will wander as you are cutting, and you will have difficulty staying on the pattern line. It will also flex from side to side, making for irregular or angled cuts. If you press too hard on a loose blade, it will usually snap.

A blade that has too much tension is much more susceptible to breaking. It also tends to pull out of the blade holders.

In general, it is better to make the blade too tight rather than too loose. As you become more practiced, you will learn how to adjust the tension of your blade correctly.

Squaring Your Table

Most scroll saws have an adjustable table that allows you to make cuts at different angles. There are times when you want your saw set at an angle, but most cutting is done with the blade perpendicular to the table. This means the table and the blade meet and create an exact 90°-angle. If the table is even slightly off-square, your cuts will be angled. This interferes with puzzle pieces, intarsia, segmentation, and many other scrolling projects. There are several ways to make sure your table is square.

Ensure your blade and table create a 90°-angle using a square.

Small Square Method: There are many different types of squares available—ranging from expensive bronze machinist's squares to inexpensive plastic drafting squares. As long as it is accurate, it doesn't matter what material it is made from. Set the square flat on the saw table against a blade that has been inserted and tensioned. Adjust the table to form a 90°-angle to the blade.

Cutting-through Method: Simply saw through a piece of scrap wood at least ¾"-thick and check the angle of the cut using a square. Adjust the table until you get a perfectly square cut.

Kerf-test Method: Take a 1¾"-thick piece of scrap and cut about ¹⁄₁₆" into it. Stop the saw, and spin the wood around to the back of the blade. If the blade slips easily into the kerf, the table is square. If not, adjust the table until it does.

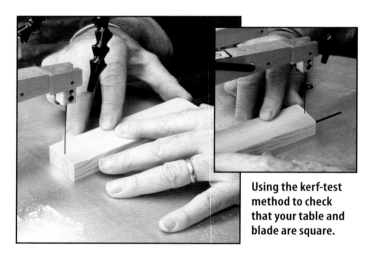

Using the kerf-test method to check that your table and blade are square.

General Scrolling Tips

For the most part, cut the delicate sections first. There are two main reasons for this. First, if you make an error that can't be easily fixed, you haven't invested a lot of time in the piece. Second, these areas tend to be fragile—the more wood you have supporting the project while cutting these areas, the better. It is a good idea to replace the scrap you cut out and tape it back in place with blue painters' tape while you continue cutting other areas.

Let the saw and blade do the work. Don't force the blade to cut—it is harder to control and tends to bend the blade, giving you beveled cuts. Run the saw at a comfortable speed. Slow down the saw in delicate areas, but increase the speed when cutting thick wood, long straight lines, or long sweeping curves.

Keep an eye on your blade and replace it when it starts to burn the wood or it doesn't seem to cut as well. Blades are inexpensive and changing a blade is quicker and easier than sanding off scorch marks. An exception is black cherry, which is known for burning even with new blades. Using tape will help to lubricate the blade and minimize burning when cutting thick or hard woods.

Sanding the surface before scrolling makes finishing easier in the long run.

Sanding Tips

It is better to sand before you cut—it is easy to damage fragile sections if you try to sand after cutting.

Start with coarse sandpaper (80-grit) and use progressively finer grits until you achieve the surface you want. After cutting, you may want to hand-sand the project lightly with 220-grit sandpaper to remove any burrs created by the cutting.

Stack Cutting

Stack cutting lets you cut several pieces of a project— or even several projects—at one time. You attach several blanks together, and cut them as one unit. There are many methods to attach the pieces together.

Use double stick tape in the corners to attach pieces for stack cutting.

Double-sided Tape: Use small pieces of double-sided tape in the corners between layers. This method is not recommended when cutting inlay projects as the layers can't have any space between them in order for the inlay to fit correctly.

Hot-melt Glue: Attach two or more blanks together with a dot of hot-melt glue on each side.

Spray Adhesive: Use spray adhesive (the kind used to attach the pattern to the blank) to each layer, following the manufacturer's instructions. We recommend spraying both sides of a sheet of paper with the adhesive and inserting the paper between the layers to be stack cut. You will be able to separate the pieces more easily than if you spray the adhesive directly on the wood.

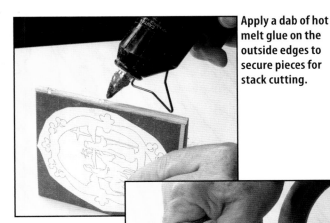

Apply a dab of hot melt glue on the outside edges to secure pieces for stack cutting.

Apply tape around the perimeter of the layers to stack cut.

Painter's Tape: Line all the layers up and wrap a layer of painter's tape around the outside edge. You can also wrap the whole stack in tape for extra stability. Clear packaging tape works as well.

Brads or Small Nails: Drive brads or small finish nails into as many waste areas as you can. Make sure the nails don't protrude below the surface of the wood—otherwise they may scratch the table surface or catch on the table and interfere with your cutting. The best thing to do is to cut any overhanging nails off as close to the surface as you can; then sand it flush. When stack cutting plywood (hardwoods tend to split with this method), some scrollers recommend nailing on top of an anvil or piece of sheet metal to keep any protruding nails flush with the wood.

Brads or nails are driven in the waste areas to secure layers for stack cutting.

Scroll Saw Blades

It is impossible for us to recommend a certain blade, but it is important for you to be familiar with the different types. Try several different brands, types and sizes to get a feel for how each blade cuts. Deciding which blade to use on a particular project is a choice that depends on the type of project, type of wood and your personal preferences.

Blade Sizes: Scroll saw blades are commonly available in sizes that range from #3/0 to #12. The smaller the number, the smaller the blade. A #3/0 (pronounced three "ought") blade is considered a jewelers' blade and is used for fine detail work. Sizes progress to a #1/0, #0 and continue through #12. A #7 blade is fairly large and is usually used for less precise perimeter cuts. Larger blades also produce larger kerfs. A kerf is the cut or channel made by the blade.

Most blades fall into one of eight categories. (Excerpted from John A. Nelson's *Scroll Saw Workbook.*)

Pin-end Blades: These blades are very wide and have pins in the end that hold the blade in the clamps. They are essentially a small version of the standard hand coping saw blade. Since the blades are bigger and have pins on the end, these blades can't be used for delicate fretwork or veining.

Standard-tooth Blades: The teeth in these blades are all the same size and distance apart. There are both metal-cutting and wood-cutting blades.

Skip-tooth Blades: These are similar to the standard-tooth blades, but every other tooth is missing. The space between the teeth is much wider, which keeps the blade cooler and allows the saw to clear out more saw dust. These blades are good for beginners because they cut relatively smoothly, and quickly.

Double-tooth Blades: These blades are similar to the skip-tooth blades but have a large space between sets of two teeth. They cut slightly slower, but clear out the sawdust better and leave a very smooth cut.

Reverse Skip-tooth Blades: This is the same as the skip-tooth blade except the last few bottom teeth point upward to help prevent splintering or tear-out on the bottom of the cut. With the arm in its highest position, be sure the reverse teeth are slightly above the top of the table when installing this type of blade.

Precision-ground Blades: Skip-tooth blades with smaller teeth ground to shape as opposed to simply filed. They are sharper, cut a straighter line, and leave a smoother surface. Precision-ground blades tend to cut aggressively, so beginners may have trouble using them.

Spiral Blades: With teeth all the way around, spiral blades allow you to cut in any direction without rotating your workpiece. Popular for portrait-style cutting or cutting projects that are too large to be rotated. The width of the saw cut is greater and the cut is rougher. They do not allow you to cut tight, sharp corners.

Crown-tooth Blades: These blades have teeth shaped like a crown with space between each tooth. They are reversible—there is no upside down. They cut wood a little slower than other blades, but are good for cutting plastic or acrylic.

Creating an Auxiliary Table

Most scroll saws on the market have an opening in the table and around the blade that is much larger than necessary. This design often causes small and delicate fretwork to break off on the downward stroke of the blade. An easy solution is to add a wooden auxiliary table to the top of the metal table on your saw.

To make an auxiliary table, choose a piece of ¼" to ⅜" plywood similar to the size of your saw's current table. We recommend that you make the table larger than what you think you will need in the future.

Next, set the auxiliary table on top of the metal table. From the underside of the metal table, use a pencil to mark the location where the blade will feed through. Then, turn the auxiliary table over and drill a ¹⁄₁₆"- to ⅛"-diameter hole or a hole slightly larger than the blade you will be using.

Finally, apply a few strips of double-sided carpet tape to the metal table on each side of the blade. Firmly press the auxiliary table onto the double-sided carpet tape, making sure the blade is centered in the hole.

Cutting Tips and Techniques

If it is your first time cutting with a scroll saw, be sure to make some test cuts before you start a project. It's important to be aware that some blades don't cut in line with the arm. Instead, most blades cut off to the right.

The blade manufacturing process is the cause. If you very lightly run your finger up the left and right sides of the blade—without the saw running—you will notice the blade has a burr on the right side. Though the burr is normally

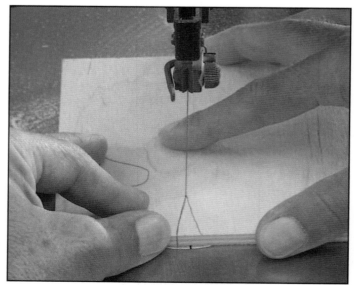

To make a tighter "V" cut, back out of the kerf and turn the blade around. Let the teeth cut into the waste area.

With a ruler lying on the line, we really see how far off the blade is cutting.

on the right, there are exceptions: crown-tooth blades can be used to cut from either end, and the precision-ground blades don't have this burr. The burr can be problematic because it makes the right side of the blade cut better.

Try cutting a piece of wood by feeding it straight into the blade, aligned with the center of the top arm. Scroll about ½" to ¾" into the wood. Notice how the blade cuts off to the right. Leave the wood in place on the saw table. Now, lay a ruler along the cut line the blade just made. Notice that it points off and to the left side of the rear of the saw (see top). Move yourself around the saw until you are looking straight down the ruler. You should be about 3" to 4" to the right of the center of the saw. Remember this position. From your new position, take that same piece of wood and try cutting into a straight line by pushing it straight into the blade. Notice how much easier it is to follow the line. From this position, we can actually feed the wood straight at the blade, and it really follows the line.

Just before you cut your project, you may want to consider the following things:

- Some scrollers recommend applying a coat of paste wax on the top surface of your table to reduce drag on the work piece.

- Look over the pattern lines. If the pattern lines are thick, pick a cutting strategy and stick to it—that is, always cut inside the line or outside the line or straight through the middle.

- If you get the pattern on the wood and determine that the pattern lines are too thin, it may be helpful to trace the pattern with a red pen or pencil to make it easier to see. Magnification can be another aid when working with these types of patterns.

- Always measure and double-check your wood. Especially double-check any parts that fit together. While ¼" oak and ¼" plywood are both labeled as the same size, there can be differences of hundredths of an inch that can affect how your project fits together. Adjust your cutting strategy accordingly because the type of wood you use, whether you adhere or trace the pattern, and any size changes you make to the pattern are just some things that can affect how you need to cut the pattern lines of a project.

When you cut your project, try to keep the following tips in mind:

- As you cut, look ahead of the blade. Doing so allows you to return to the line if you start to stray from it. Never back up to get back on track. Instead, gradually return to the line as you cut so that you don't interrupt the continuous cut of the blade.

- Generally, cut delicate sections first. There are two main reasons for this. First, if you make an error that can't be easily fixed, you haven't invested a lot of time in the project. Second, these areas tend to be fragile—the more wood you have supporting the project while cutting these areas, the better. It is a good idea to replace the scrap you cut out and tape it back in place with blue painter's tape while you continue cutting other areas.

- Let the saw and blade do the work. Don't force the blade to cut—it is harder to control and tends to bend the blade, giving you beveled cuts. Run the saw at a comfortable speed. Slow down the saw in delicate areas, but increase the speed when cutting thick wood, long straight lines, or long sweeping curves.

- Keep an eye on your blade and replace it when it starts to burn the wood or it doesn't seem to cut as well. Blades are inexpensive and changing a blade is quicker and easier than sanding off scorch marks. Using tape will help lubricate the blade and minimize burning when cutting thick or hard woods.

- Good hand position is key to successful cutting. Remember to apply enough, but not too much, pressure to the wood. Your hand position must also allow you to move the wood around the blade freely. Remember, you are feeding the wood at the blade, not vice versa. Place one hand on each side of the wood. For some, it's easiest to hook the tip of the thumb and a couple of fingers over the edges of the wood, and use the remaining fingers to apply the downward holding pressure.

- Always keep your fingers off to the sides of the blade path, so that if your finger slides, it does not slide into the blade. On some cuts, such as when you are trying to shave off a narrow strip, the blade could jump out of the cut, allowing the wood to jump, and your finger that was in the path would go right into the blade.

- For making smooth curves, have a pivot point for your wood. When making curves and turns, one hand will be the stationary pivot and the other hand will do the turning. Place the index fingertip from either hand on the wood and apply enough pressure so the wood will pivot around that finger. Use the thumb and remaining fingers of that hand to hold the wood down on the table. Then, turn the wood with your other hand. The direction of the curve will dictate which hand is the pivot and which hand does the turning. It is easier to switch pivot hands to pivot guide the wood through the curves that flow in the opposite direction.

- Many find it easier to cut curves by picking an imaginary point about ¹⁄₁₆" in front of the cutting path of the blade. The curved line being cut should always be in line with that the imaginary point. This seems to make it easier for the blade to follow the line.

- Corners are generally created by cutting to one side, spinning the wood until the blade is in line with the new direction, and feeding again. To hold the blade in place while we spin the wood, we'll use the sides and back of the blade because they do not cut. As you approach the corner, stop feeding the wood at the blade. Then, apply slight pressure to the side of the blade at the outside of the corner—just enough to help maintain the blade's position. As you turn the wood to the new direction, maintain pressure on the side, then the back, of the blade until the new direction line to be cut is aligned with the blade. By keeping the sides or the back of the blade in contact with the wood, it's easier to keep the blade in the correct position for the new cutting direction.

- For tight V-shaped notches, cut down to the bottom of the V, then back up a little into the kerf you just cut. Use the side, then the back of the blade against the save piece, which is the part of the project you are saving, to maintain blade position and flip the wood around 180°, so the blade is now cutting in the opposite direction. The teeth will have to cut into the scrap part of the wood, as you flipped the wood around to reverse the blade's direction. Now, back the blade down into the end of the cut, at the bottom of the V. Turn the wood to the new direction, and cut out the following new line. You should have just created a nice tight V that does not show those telltale marks of cutting in from both directions.

- Try sanding off any small nibs using the burr on the right side of the blade. Every time you start a cut and finish at the same place, there is a chance to leave a small nib of wood at that point, which will need to be sanded off later. You may need to slightly angle the blade as if you were trying to just shave a little wood off the edge, but you will pick up this trick easily after doing it a few times.

- As you cut, watch for chattering, which happens when the teeth of the blade catch on the wood, drawing it up and down with the blade's movement. Chattering is not only annoying, but it can be potentially fatal to your project. First, it can make the blade wander off the line. Second, delicate pieces can break off when the wood bangs against the table.

Veining

Veining is a simple technique that will bring a lifelike appearance to your projects. The veins of a leaf or the folds of clothing will look more realistic when this technique is applied.

To vein, choose a thin blade (usually smaller than #7) and saw all solid black lines, as indicated on the pattern. You will be able to vein some areas of the pattern by sawing inward from the outside edge; in other areas, you will need to drill a tiny blade entry hole for the blade. If you wish to make a project easier, simply omit the veining.

Veining can give your projects a lifelike appearance. Many times veining areas will be as simple as cutting inward from the outside edge.

Tips and Techniques for Clock Inserts

If you have a project that requires a clock insert, first make sure you have a good friction fit. Clock inserts fit through friction, so it is important that you check and double-check the size of the insert and the hole as you go. Squaring the blade is important for this step because a cut that's too far off can mean having an insert that doesn't fit. The need for a friction fit is also why many of the contributors who use routers or sandpaper to round the edges of their projects warn not to round the clock insert hole. The rounding of the edge can inhibit the fit.

When you are purchasing an insert, be careful that you choose the correct insert size for your project. Also, if you choose to enlarge or reduce a project or choose to use a different insert with the same size project, make sure you make any necessary adjustments before you begin cutting.

Sawing Thin Woods

Thin hardwoods or plywoods can be difficult to work with because they're prone to breaking. The following suggestions should help to eliminate or reduce this problem.

If you have a variable speed saw, reduce the speed to half or three-quarters of high speed.

If you do not have a variable speed saw, it will help to stack cut two or more layers of material to prevent breakage.

With any material, it is important that your feed rate and blade speed match so that burn marks won't appear on the wood. If you prefer to feed the wood into the blade slowly, set your saw on a slow setting or try using a smaller blade with more teeth per inch (TPI) to slow down the speed at which the blade is cutting. On the other hand if you prefer to feed the wood into the blade quickly, choose a fast setting for your saw or try using a blade with fewer TPI.

Finishing Techniques

Finishing can be done before or after you assemble your project. For many pieces, especially those with a fair amount of fretwork, it is easier to apply the finish prior to assembling. If you finish the piece before assembly, you also have more options for using contrasting stains.

If you make your project from hardwood, try dipping it in a dishpan (or a similar container) filled with a penetrating oil, such as Watco or tung. Then, allow the excess oil to drain back into the pan, and follow the manufacturer's instructions. If you have chosen to use plywood on any parts of your project, try using a matching shade of stain to give an appealing look to the finished project. As a final finish step once the pieces have dried, use a clear, Varathane-type spray for a protective coating.

If you are going to spray paint a piece, include a breakaway tab into the design (see below). This gives you a place to hold the work while you paint. It is easily removed later with a knife.

No matter what finish you use, remember to plan for the final display of your piece. An indoor display does not need any special finish, but a sign or weather vane will need special attention to withstand the elements.

Incorporating a breakaway tab into a design will provide a place to hold the piece while applying a spray finish.

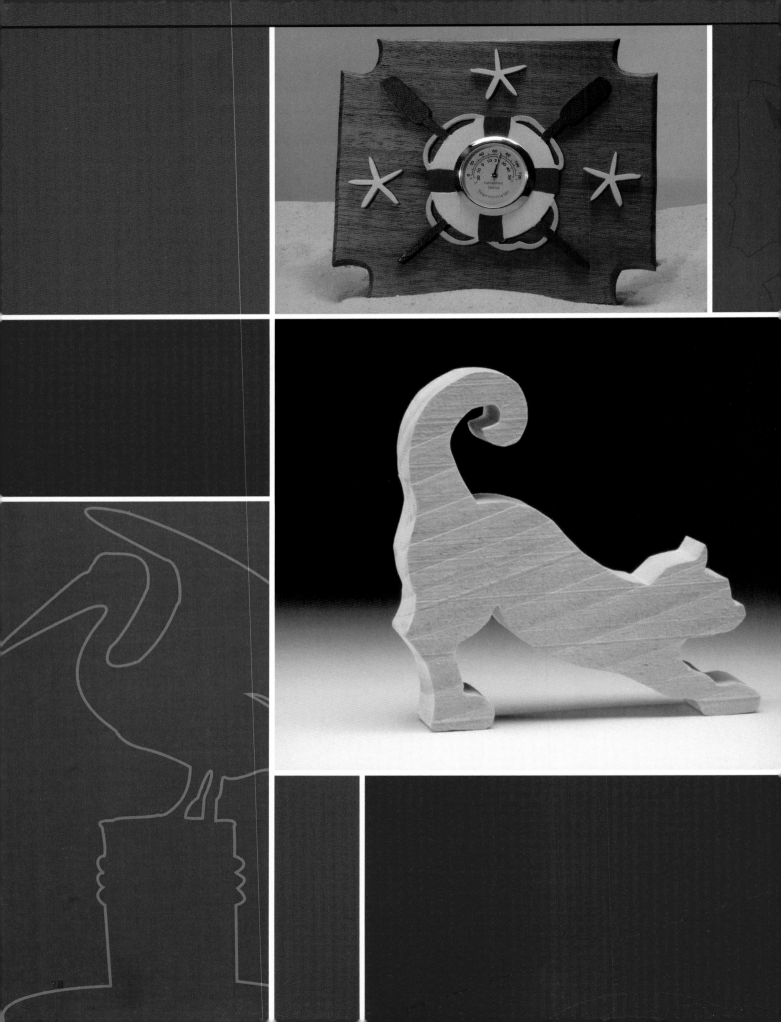

Beginning Patterns

If you're just starting out, try these simple patterns to get used to the feel of the blade and the saw and to practice some of the common shapes and techniques you'll use in many projects. While these projects are simply meant as practice, you could certainly turn any of these patterns into ornaments and projects when you achieve the look you want. Don't be afraid to experiment and use your imagination!

Bell and Christmas Tree
Easy-to-Scroll Patterns for Beginners

If you're a "new blade" to scrolling, use these patterns to help you grow comfortable with your scroll saw. They don't have any inside cuts, so there's no need to worry about changing and threading the blade.

To Cut the Patterns

Step 1: Attach a photocopy of the pattern to the wood. Use some sort of temporary bond adhesive. If using spray, do not spray the wood. If you do, removing the pattern is very difficult.

Step 2: Insert your blade so the teeth point downward and check the tension. Pluck the blade as you would a string on a stringed instrument. You should hear a crisp "ping" and not a "plunk." Adjust tension as needed.

Step 3: Position the work piece so you are making your first cut at the "In" line. Turn the saw on and have fun. Don't worry if you wander off the pattern line. Once the pattern is removed, you'll be the only one who knew you didn't follow it exactly. To get sharp points on the tree, follow the line on the pattern to loop beyond the point.

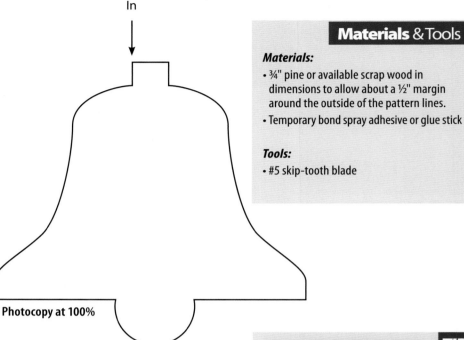

In

Photocopy at 100%

Materials & Tools

Materials:
- ¾" pine or available scrap wood in dimensions to allow about a ½" margin around the outside of the pattern lines.
- Temporary bond spray adhesive or glue stick

Tools:
- #5 skip-tooth blade

REMEMBER THESE THINGS   TIP

- *As you cut, keep firm, but not white-knuckled, pressure on the wood. The blade sometimes grabs the wood and smacks it up and down on the saw table rapidly. This is called "chatter" and can be a little scary the first few times it happens.*

- *Keep your arms and shoulders relaxed.*

- *When you make your first cut, you may notice you can't seem to cut straight. It may be the blade. All but precision ground teeth blades have burrs on one side that cause the blade to wander to one side of the pattern line. To compensate, cut into a scrap piece of wood and see what direction the blade is cutting. Then, align your body position with the line, so as you push the blade into the wood, you're cutting straight.*

- *Most important: Have fun!*

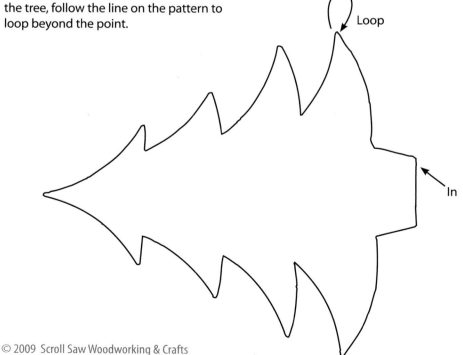

Loop

In

Cross and Watering Can

Practice Cutting and Making Sharp Points

In this exercise, we're focusing not only on the basics of cutting but also on making sharp points.

Cutting the Patterns

Step 1: Attach a photocopy of the pattern to the wood. Use temporary bond adhesive. Your wood should be about the size of the border around each pattern. If you decide to use spray adhesive, be sure to spray the pattern and not the wood. Spraying the wood will make pattern removal difficult.

Step 2: Insert your blade, with the teeth pointing downward. Check the tension and adjust as necessary. Make sure the blade is at a 90° angle to the table.

Step 3: Position your work piece. Make your first cut at the "In" line for the Cross and at the blade entry hole for the Watering Can. Turn the saw on, relax, and have fun.

TIPS

• Before you begin to cut, plan a cutting strategy. In the case of the watering can, remember to make the interior cut first, so you have more to hang on to. Drill a blade entry hole, thread the blade through and begin cutting.

• To make the sharp points on the cross, cut each arc first. Once you have cut all four arcs, cut in toward the body of the cross along each of the eight straight lines. Using this cutting strategy will help to ensure the points are sharp and not rounded.

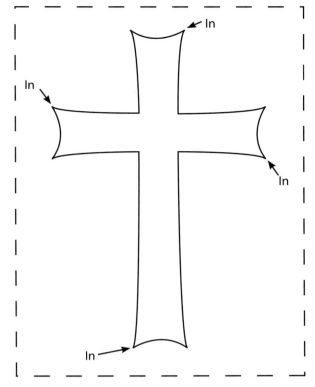

Photocopy at 100%

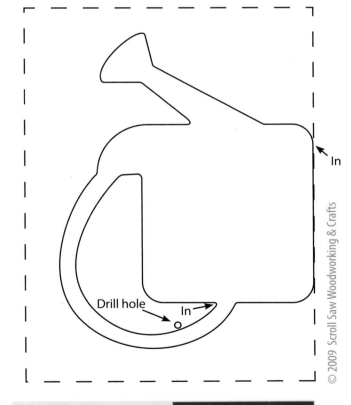

Materials & Tools

Materials:
- ¾" x 3" x 4" pine
- Temporary bond spray adhesive or glue stick

Tools:
- #5 skip-tooth blade
- Drill with a ⅛"-diameter bit

Scroll a Curious Cat
Practice Cutting Curves

In this exercise, we're focusing on cutting curves.

Cutting the Pattern

Step 1: Attach a photocopy of the pattern to the wood. Use temporary bond adhesive. Your wood should be at least ¼" larger than the pattern. For this project, a 4½" x 5½" piece of wood will give you a lot of wood around the edges to hold on to. If you decide to use spray adhesive, be sure to spray the pattern and not the wood. Spraying the wood will make pattern removal difficult.

Step 2: Insert the blade into the blade clamps. Make sure the teeth are pointing downward. Check the tension and adjust as necessary. You should hear a crisp "ping" and not a "plunk" when you pluck the blade. Make sure the blade is at a 90˚ angle to the table.

Step 3: Turn the saw on. Then, relax and have fun.

Materials & Tools

Materials:
- ¾" x 4½" x 5½" pine
- Temporary bond spray adhesive or glue stick

Tools:
- #5 skip-tooth blade

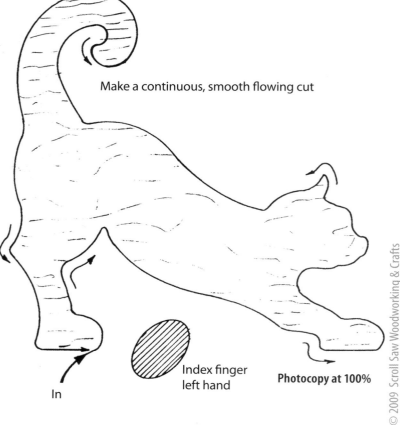

Make a continuous, smooth flowing cut

Index finger left hand

In

Photocopy at 100%

© 2009 Scroll Saw Woodworking & Crafts

Maple Leaf Pattern
Practice Cutting Sharp Corners

This exercise focuses on the different methods you can use to make sharp corners.

Cutting the Patterns

Step 1: Attach a photocopy of the pattern to the wood. Use temporary bond spray adhesive or a glue stick. Your wood should be about the size of the border around the pattern. If you decide to use spray adhesive, be sure to spray the pattern and not the wood. Spraying the back of the pattern will help to keep the adhesive from getting into the wood grain and ruining any stain or finish you would add to the wood later. It is important to always clean and sand all adhesive off before going on with any finishing process.

Step 2: Insert the blade. Make sure the teeth are pointing downward. Check the tension and adjust as necessary. Make sure the blade is at a 90° angle to the table. Step 3: Position your work piece. Make your first cut at the "In" line for the Maple Leaf. Turn the saw on, relax, and have fun.

Step 3: Position your work piece. Make your first cut at the "In" line for the Maple Leaf. Turn the saw on, relax, and have fun.

Step 4: Cut the first corner. When you reach the first sharp corner, where the stem meets the leaf, stop pushing the wood, relax, and back off slightly. Then, rotate the wood to line up with the direction of the line and continue cutting.

Step 5: Cut the second corner. When you reach the next sharp corner, the lower right corner of the leaf, use the loop method to create a sharp point. To use this method, cut beyond the point and loop back around to cut in the direction of the line. Follow the arrowheads marked on the pattern. Use these two methods to create the rest of the sharp corners in this project.

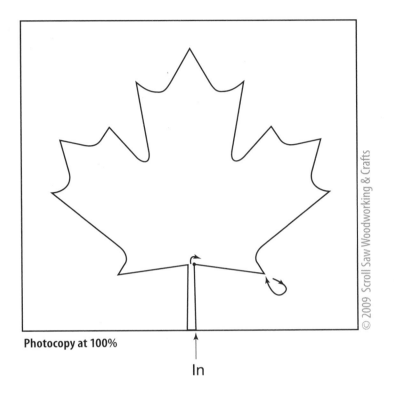

Photocopy at 100%

In

© 2009 Scroll Saw Woodworking & Crafts

Materials & Tools

Materials:
- ¾" x 3½" x 3½" pine
- Temporary bond spray adhesive or glue stick

Tools:
- #5 skip-tooth blade

Improve Your Scrolling

Simple Tricks Make a Big Difference

by Wm. Hofferth

Editor's note: If you're new to scrolling, you'll find these helpful hints useful in taking your craft to the next level. To practice those skills, we've included a pattern that can be used as the basis for several finished projects: a nautical thermometer, a clock, or a barometer.

Getting Started

- Warm up by cutting the basic staircase design (Figure A) in a scrap piece of ¾" pine. This design requires you to use all of the skills needed to cut just about any design.
- Keep a good coat of paste wax on the top surface of your table. The wax reduces the drag on your workpiece.
- Patterns can be used at any size. Reduce or enlarge them to suit on a photocopier or computer.

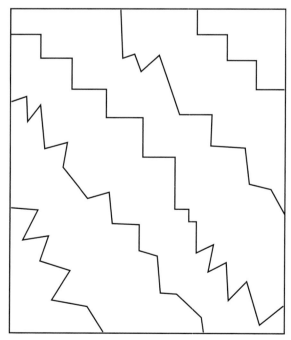

Figure A

Cutting

- Look and anticipate ahead of the blade. This allows you to regain the line if you start to stray off it.
- Never back up to get back on track! Gradually regain the line as you cut so you don't interrupt the continuous cut of the blade.
- Start an inside cut on an inside corner (Figure B). This effectively hides the point at which the cut began.
- Do not cut "off a pattern element" and continue (Figure C). This leaves a part of your project too sharp and it will chip and splinter later on. Try to exercise the moves from the staircase design to make the complete turn. This leaves more finished or burnished edges less likely to chip or break later.

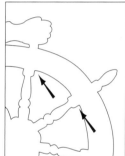

Figure B

Figure C

Blades

- Use a #5 scroll saw blade for wood, and a #2 scroll saw blade for paper.

Material

- Do not cut material that is too thick or too thin. Finding the right thickness or stack of material is very important for success in scrolling. If the wood is too thick, you will be frustrated with blade breakage, burning of the material, and difficulty in getting through the project. If the wood is too thin, it presents another set of problems, including not enough resistance to the blade, which makes it very difficult to turn and to stay on the lines.

Finishing

- If you are going to spray paint a piece, include a break-away tab into the design (Figure D). This gives you a place to hold the work while you paint. It is easily removed later with the score of a knife.
- Plan for the final display of your piece. An indoor display does not need any special finish, but a sign or weather vane will need special attention to withstand the elements.

Figure D

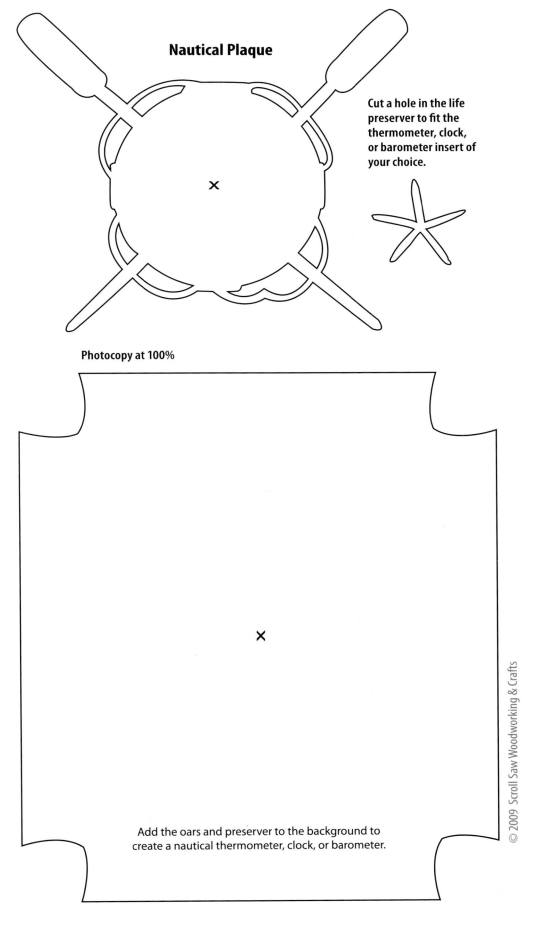

Nautical Plaque

Cut a hole in the life preserver to fit the thermometer, clock, or barometer insert of your choice.

Photocopy at 100%

Add the oars and preserver to the background to create a nautical thermometer, clock, or barometer.

© 2009 Scroll Saw Woodworking & Crafts

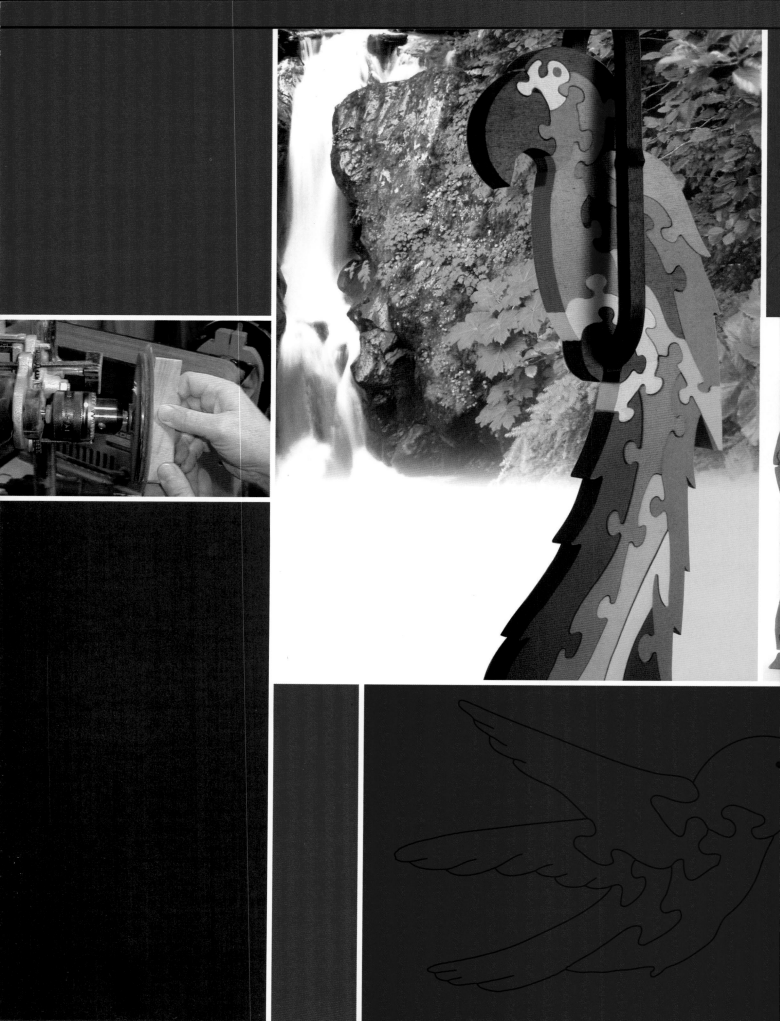

Puzzles and Toys

The scroll saw is an excellent tool for creating puzzles and toys of all varieties. Following are just a few examples. These projects can also be finished in a number of different ways, allowing you to experiment with everything from paints and colored stains to natural stains and clear finishes.

Hanging Macaw Puzzle

From the Amazon jungles to your home

By John A. Nelson

When my wife, Joyce, and I traveled to Africa, there were birds everywhere. We thought for sure when we went to Peru that we would see lots of birds, too. As it turns out, that wasn't the case. The ones we had the best looks at were residents at lodges where we stayed. One morning, we woke up to see three macaws on a ceiling rafter looking down at us as we slept. What a way to wake up!

This hanging macaw puzzle reminds me of our Peru trip. For you, it's a nice eye-catcher for your craft booth or home. Plus, if you know someone who has an itch for a pet bird, as Joyce did when she found out her twin sister got one, make this puzzle instead. It's a lot less mess and there are no vet bills. (It's a great puzzle for kids—just don't make the support and use child-safe paints.)

Step 1: Cut the blanks. Cut two pieces, one for the body and one for the support, to overall size.

Step 2: Attach the pattern. Use temporary bond spray adhesive. Make sure you spray the pattern and not the wood.

Step 3: Make the outside cut of the parrot. Use the #5 blade. Complete the cutting by making all of the interior cuts for the puzzle pieces.

Step 4: Sand. Lightly sand each puzzle piece to remove all burrs.

Step 5: Cut the support. Glue the pattern to the piece of wood for the support and cut it out with the #5 blade. Make sure the dimension labeled "x" on the pattern is the same thickness as the body.

Step 6: Decide on a finish. The macaw can be painted, though it is better to use wood stains. I recommend fully transparent intermixable wood stains, such as Woodburst, because paint is too thick. (The macaw shown in the photograph was painted.)

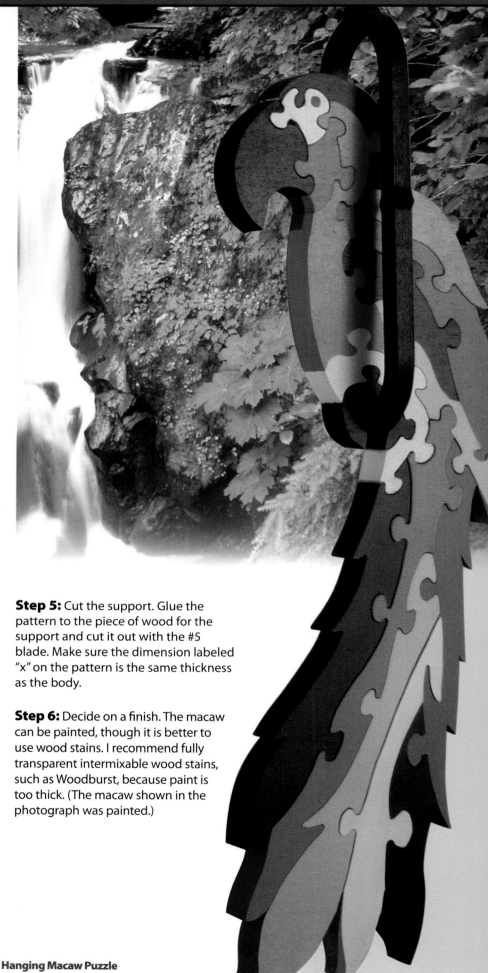

Materials:

- ⅝" x 8" x 17" pine (body)
  Note: ¾" can be used. Make sure the dimension on the notch is widened.
- ½" x 2½" x 8" pine (support)
- Temporary bond spray adhesive
- Sandpaper, fine grit
- Eyebolt, small
- Wood stains, colors of choice, or paint with bright colors

Tools:

- #5 skip-tooth blade

Step 7: Mix colors. Pour the stain into a paper cup or other suitable container for easy application or mixing colors.

Step 8: Add color. Dip a rag into a cup and apply generously to all surfaces. You can use artists' brushes, if you wish. Wipe off excess by dragging the towel with the grain. Let the piece dry for 48 hours.

Step 9: Add the eye bolt to the support.

Step 10: Assemble the puzzle. Then, attach it to the support. Now if we could only get the darn thing to talk!

Colors

A = Black
B = White
C = Dark blue
D = Medium blue
E = Light blue
F = Light orange
G = Dark yellow
H = Light yellow

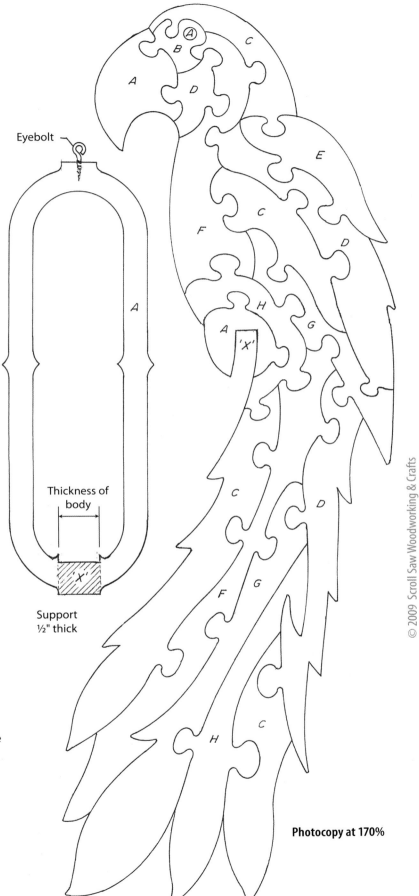

Eyebolt

Thickness of body

Support
½" thick

© 2009 Scroll Saw Woodworking & Crafts

Photocopy at 170%

Balancing Hummingbird

An unusual freestanding puzzle

By Judy Peterson

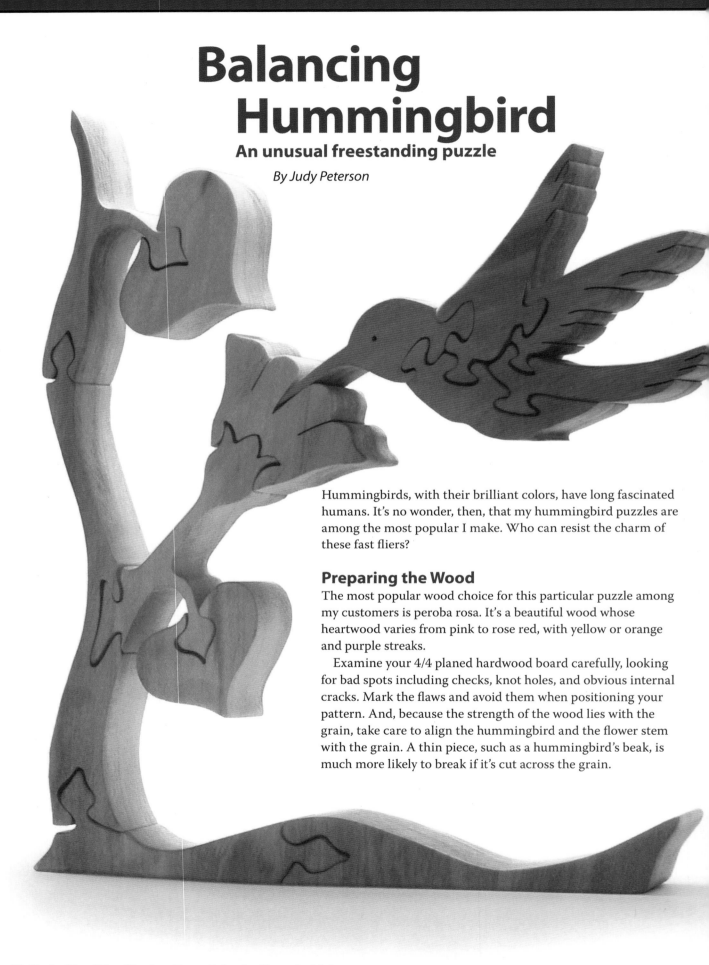

Hummingbirds, with their brilliant colors, have long fascinated humans. It's no wonder, then, that my hummingbird puzzles are among the most popular I make. Who can resist the charm of these fast fliers?

Preparing the Wood

The most popular wood choice for this particular puzzle among my customers is peroba rosa. It's a beautiful wood whose heartwood varies from pink to rose red, with yellow or orange and purple streaks.

Examine your 4/4 planed hardwood board carefully, looking for bad spots including checks, knot holes, and obvious internal cracks. Mark the flaws and avoid them when positioning your pattern. And, because the strength of the wood lies with the grain, take care to align the hummingbird and the flower stem with the grain. A thin piece, such as a hummingbird's beak, is much more likely to break if it's cut across the grain.

Glue the pattern to the board with temporary bond spray adhesive. Remember to spray the paper and not the board. I use a glue box to help confine the overspray.

Drill the eyeholes before you start cutting. Though I use a small bit in a drill press, you should use the tool that works for you. You can use a regular drill or a drill bit in a rotary power tool, like a Dremel. Because you will be creating the holes on both sides of the head with one drilling action, be sure your drill or rotary tool is perpendicular to the wood surface. If it's not, you'll end up with eyes in different positions on the two sides of the head.

Making the Cuts

I have a preference for cutting on the right-hand side of the blade. All of my patterns are set up to be cut that way. I use a standard #7 or #7 reverse-tooth blade. The kerf is wide enough to allow the pieces to slide in and out easily. At the same time, the puzzles hang together well. (Choice of blade, however, is ultimately up to you.)

The first cut on this pattern begins at the top portion of the vertical piece. Next, cut the first piece of the base.

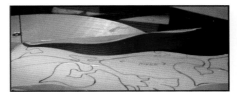
The first cut of the pattern.

The puzzle stands better when there is a slight curve in the base.

Experience proves the puzzle stands more securely if the base is slightly curved. With the base complete, continue cutting. As each piece is cut free, remove that piece from the saw table and peel off the pattern.

After cutting both pieces of the base, proceed with the stalk. The deep V in the petals is the trickiest spot in this pattern. You need to cut all of the way to the bottom of the V and back out about halfway between the bottom of the V and the curved portion of the petal. Turn the piece of wood completely around at this point by cutting into the waste. Now, you can back the blade up to the end of the V and proceed up the side of the next petal. (See Illustration 1 for complete cutting instructions.)

Look at the place on the stalk where the top piece connects to the piece below it. These are the narrowest and weakest parts of this pattern. Follow the lines on the pattern as precisely as possible to avoid breakage.

When you've finished the stalk, petals, and flower, you're ready to cut the hummingbird. I start at the tip of the beak, cut around the top of the head, and cut out the top piece of the wing. Finish cutting out the bird. As

After the stalk and petals have been cut, it's on to the bird next. Begin at the tip of the beak, cut around the head, and finish by cutting out the top piece of the wing.

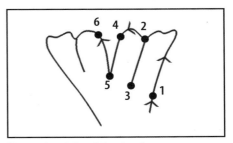

Illustration 1: Petal Cutting Strategy.
To achieve a clean narrow cut in the main V of the petal, follow this cutting strategy. Start at 1 and cut in the direction of the arrow. Go past 2 and stop at 3. Carefully pull your workpiece toward you until the blade is at 2. Cut forward again past 4 to 5. Again, pull the workpiece carefully back to 4. With the saw running, turn the workpiece 180° counterclockwise. Then, pull the workpiece carefully back to 5. Cut up to 6 and finish the other petals.

I cut each piece free and remove its pattern, I reassemble the puzzle nearby.

Now that you've cut the puzzle, notice the two parts (the bird and the stalk/base) are independently interlocking. That is, as long as you hold the bird straight up and down, you can turn it 360° and it doesn't fall apart.

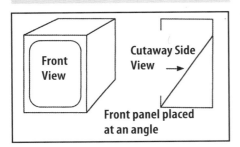

Sanding

These puzzles are meant to be handled, and smooth feels better. Put another way, silky means sales in the art show booth! I do much of the sanding with a drill held in place by a drill stand. At this point, my disk sander is chucked into the drill. The sander can be used for both flat and edge sanding. Sand the interior cuts only enough to remove wood fibers where you've cut two pieces apart. Feel to make sure the surfaces are smooth.

I round off the sharp corners with a Sand-O-Flex. This tool effectively sands rounded surfaces without gouging.

To do both flat and edge sanding, I chuck my disc sander into a drill held in place by a drill stand. Here, I am flat sanding.

Here, I am edge sanding.

The Sand-O-Flex in motion.

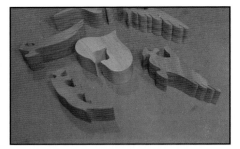

After Sand-O-Flexing, the rough edges are now smooth.

After dipping the pieces in an oil bath, let them drip dry on a paper towel. (Because the oil fumes are volatile, the towels should dry thoroughly in a well-ventilated area before you dispose of them properly.)

The puzzle, after an oil bath.

It has eight slots for sandpaper, and each of the eight pieces of sandpaper is scored into ⅛" strips, giving you 64 "little fingers" to get into tiny crevices. The length of the sandpaper is adjustable. I can do large projects with long strips, and then reel in the sandpaper to do small projects. (To find Sand-O-Flex in your area, call Merit Abrasives, 800-421-1936.) If you're careful, you can get the same result

CUTTING SAFETY   **TIP**

One of the questions I'm most frequently asked is, "Do you cut all the way around the outside and then cut out the pieces?" The answer is always, "No!" It is both safer and easier to always leave a piece of the scrap to hang on to for your final cut. This is especially important when doing small pieces like hummingbird parts.

with another flap sander. To protect my fingers, I use rubber fingertips.

The last step is to oil the pieces. Pour the oil in a container. You may want to use rubber gloves to protect your hands. Drop the pieces into the oil, then remove them and let them drip dry on a paper towel. As necessary, wipe the oil off. The more cut-line detail there is in a piece, the more attention it needs at this step. After drying all of the pieces that need it, reassemble the puzzle and let it air-dry overnight. Remember, oil fumes are extremely volatile. Let the paper towels dry thoroughly in a spot with good air circulation before discarding them.

Materials & Tools

Materials:
- One 4/4" hardwood board at least 10" X 8"
- Temporary bond spray adhesive (I use Duro All-Purpose Spray Adhesive)
- Sanding disks to fit your disk sander —I sand to 220 grit
- Rubber Finger Tips (or other fingertip protection)
- Clear Danish oil (I use General Finishes—Natural)
- Rubber gloves
- Paper towels

Tools:
- Drill press, rotary power tool or regular electric drill with ¹⁄₁₆" or smaller bit
- #7 standard or #7 reverse tooth blades
- Disk sander
- Sand-O-Flex or another flap sander
- Container to hold the oil

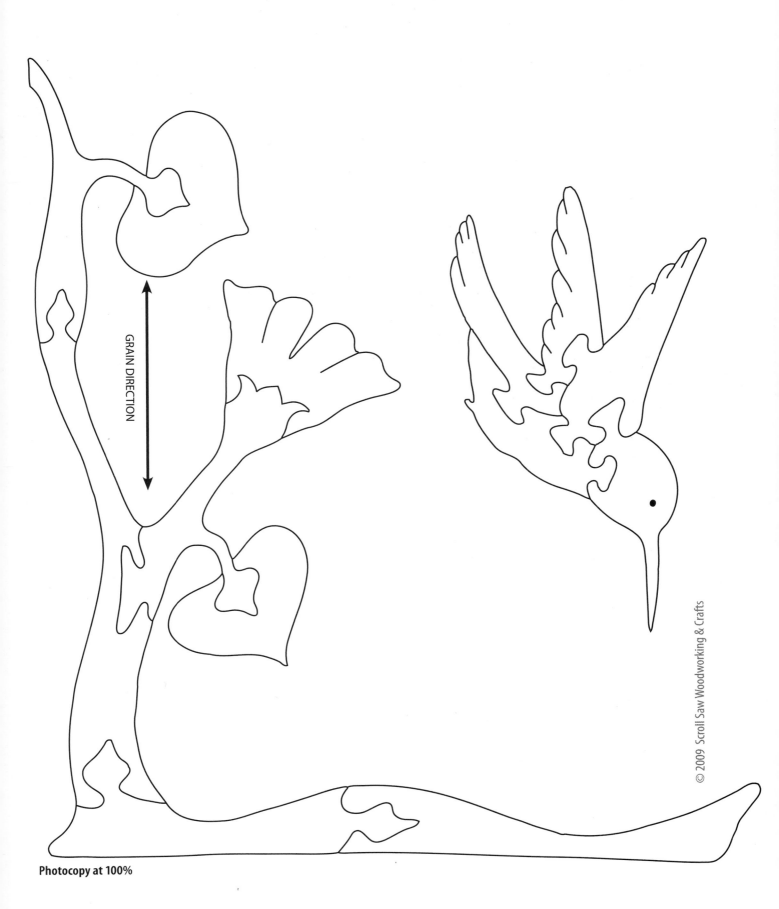

GRAIN DIRECTION

Photocopy at 100%

© 2009 Scroll Saw Woodworking & Crafts

A Toy from the Land Down Under

You and your child can make Hoppy the Kangaroo

By Jim Stirling

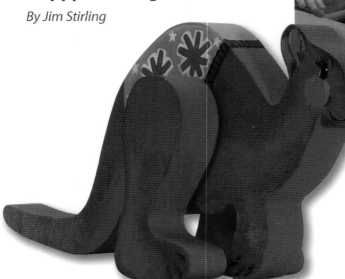

Children enjoy playing with Hoppy the Kangaroo whether it is painted or not. A finish for your kangaroo is an optional step if you use medium-density fiberboard. Donna Lloyd painted the version shown here.

If you want to work with a child to make a unique and inexpensive toy or surprise a youngster with a gift, have a go at Hoppy the Kangaroo. Once you complete this project, the kangaroo, powered by gravity, can hop down a board. He first rocks onto his front legs so that his back legs slide forward. Then, his body moves forward, his legs go back, and he rocks onto his front legs again. And so he goes, hopping down the slope.

The kangaroo can be made easily from a piece of medium-density fiberboard (MDF). MDF is hard, does not chip out, and is excellent for making toys.

Step 1: Prepare the patterns. Make a copy of the body pattern and two copies of the leg pattern (one for the left and one for the right). Use scissors to cut around the patterns, leaving about ⅛" of paper around the outlines.

Step 2: Cut the wood. Make it about ¼" larger than the size of the patterns.

Step 3: Attach the patterns. Nestle the three pattern pieces beside each other on the wood to make the most economical use of the wood. Adhere the patterns using temporary bond spray adhesive.

Alternate: Make a template to ease replication of the toy. Glue a pattern of the body and one back leg onto thin plywood. Cut the pieces out and drill ⅛"-diameter holes to mark eyes and places to be drilled. The templates can be placed directly onto the wood and traced around with a pencil. Remember to turn the back leg piece over to get both left and right legs. A small nail can be used to mark the places to be drilled.

Step 4: Cut the two back leg pieces. Use a #9 reverse-tooth blade.

Step 5: Cut the main piece. Use the #9 reverse-tooth blade. To ensure the kangaroo will be able to move, be especially accurate cutting the belly between the back legs and on the bottom of the feet. If a child is cutting the toy, it doesn't really matter for the function of the toy if he or she strays off the line around the body as long as the other cutting mentioned in this step is accurate.

Step 6: Drill two holes. Use a ¼"-diameter bit for the inside of each of the back legs as shown on the pattern. Drill the holes ½" deep. Using a ⅜"-diameter bit, drill a hole right through the body, in the belly region, as marked on the pattern. Using a ⅛"-diameter bit, make eyes on both sides of the head.

Step 7: Cut the dowels. Using the scroll saw, cut two ¼"-diameter dowels, each 2" long. The dowels will be used to connect the back legs to the body, enabling those legs to move together.

Step 8: Sand. Once the pieces are cut and the holes drilled, sand lightly around the edges with 100-grit sandpaper.

Step 9: Paint (optional). I did not paint Hoppy, but you can. For example, you can use brown paint for a Big Red Kangaroo or gray paint for an Eastern Gray Kangaroo.

Step 10: Dowel the legs. To assemble, first hammer the dowels into the top and bottom of one leg.

Step 11: Attach the body. Holding the back leg containing the two dowels, insert the top dowel through the hole in the kangaroo's body. At the same time, the bottom dowel in the leg should fit beneath the body so the leg can swing.

Step 12: Complete the kangaroo. Next, dry-fit the other leg onto the two exposed dowels on the other side of the body. You may have to trim a little wood off the bottom of the belly so the legs can swing evenly without hitting the belly. Leave about ⅛" of play between the body and the legs.

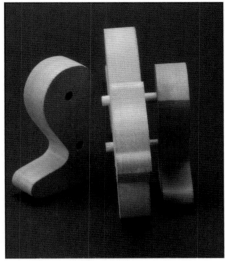

Now, it's time for the kangaroo to use his powerful back legs. Find a board about 3' long. Its surface needs to be fairly rough to provide friction so the kangaroo doesn't slide. Put the plank on an angle, place the kangaroo on the top, pull his tail back and watch him go!

Adjust the angle of the plank until the kangaroo is rocking forward and backward most efficiently. The optimum angle for each kangaroo varies, but a kid will have no trouble finding it through experimentation.

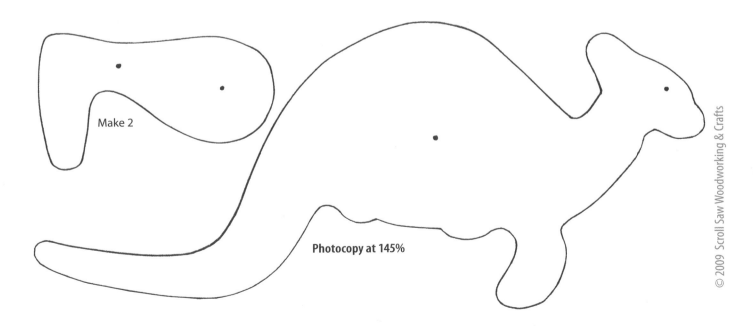

Make 2

Photocopy at 145%

© 2009 Scroll Saw Woodworking & Crafts

Wooden Gears Gizmo

Make this one just for fun

By Rick Hutcheson

Sometimes you need a project that's just for fun. This gizmo fills the bill perfectly. Not only will you enjoy the challenge of making wooden gears, but also, once it's completed, you'll be amazed by how much attention it gets from both kids and adults. People love to fiddle around with it. Add a little paint to the gears and front designs for a whole new effect.

Note: Gears depend on precision. It is better to cut outside the lines and sand down the pieces than to have gears that do not fit together. Some fitting—and patience—is required for this project.

Step 1: Cut the dowel. Cut the ¼" dowel into the lengths shown on the template page.

Step 2: Prepare for cutting. For the patterns that require multiple pieces, I stack cut two layers of plywood so both pieces are cut at the same time. This also ensures the holes in the frames are aligned with each other. Spray the patterns with temporary bond spray adhesive and apply them to the plywood.

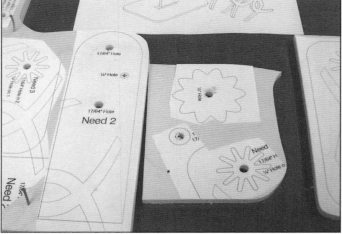

Step 3: Drill all of the holes as indicated on the patterns.

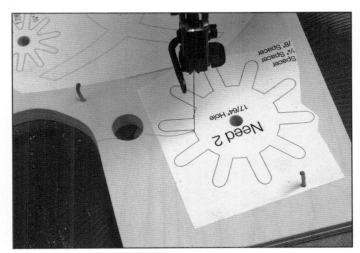

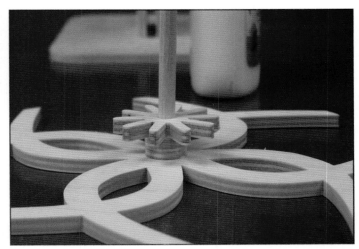

Step 4: Cut the gears. All cutting is done with a #2/0 reverse blade. When cutting the gears, the important parts are the tips and sides of each tooth. These must be smooth, so I start at the base of the tooth to get a consistent, flowing cut.

Step 5: Sand all of the pieces using 180-grit sandpaper. If you plan to paint or stain some of the parts, do it at this time, before assembling.

Step 6: Glue a ¼"-thick spacer with a ¼" hole on the end of the ¾"-long piece of ¼" dowel. Place the small gear, with the ¹⁷⁄₆₄" hole, onto the assembly. Then, glue the dowel-gear assembly into the ¼" hole in the front upright.

Step 7: Glue the uprights into the base. Make sure the holes line up. This can be done by placing dowels into the holes and rotating them to ensure they spin freely. Also, make sure they sit square to the frame face in all directions.

Step 8: Continue assembly. Lay the spinner with the ¹⁷⁄₆₄" hole on the table. Glue the ¼" and ⅛" spacers, with the ¹⁷⁄₆₄" holes, and a small gear with the ¹⁷⁄₆₄" hole together as shown. A dowel scrap can be inserted into the hole to help align the parts. It's important that the finished assembly spins freely on the dowel. If needed, the ¹⁷⁄₆₄" hole can be redrilled after the glue has dried.

Step 9: Glue the handle wheel on the end of a 2⅛"-long piece of ¼" dowel. Insert the dowel through the back upright frame. Glue one of the larger gears onto the dowel in between the two uprights. Push the dowel through the front upright. Glue one of the small gears with the ¼" hole onto the end of the dowel, leaving enough space between the gears and uprights so the assembly turns freely.

SELECTING THE RIGHT DRILL BIT   **TIP**

Some ¼" dowels do not fit tightly in a ¼"-diameter hole because they are actually undersized dowels. Drill a ¼"-diameter hole in scrap wood and test your dowels for a tight fit into the hole. You may need to use a bit that's smaller than ¼" to make a hole that results in a tight fit when you place the dowel in it. Substitute that bit size anywhere that a ¼" bit is called for to make dowel holes.

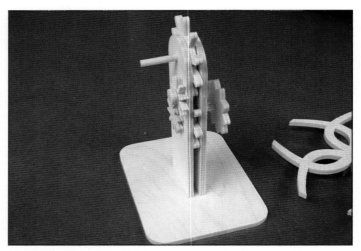

Materials & Tools

Materials:
- ¼" x 16" x 16" Baltic birch plywood
- ⅛" x 1" x 1" Baltic birch plywood
- Temporary bond spray adhesive
- ¼" dowel, 5" long
- Sandpaper, 180 grit
- Wood glue
- Finish of choice

Tools:
- Drill with ¹⁷⁄₆₄"- and ¼"-diameter drill bits
- #2/0 reverse-tooth blade

Step 10: Glue the other large gear. It goes between the uprights to the 2⅛"-long dowel inserted flush with the back of the rear upright. Again, this assembly should turn freely.

Step 11: Place the dowel-gear assembly from Step 6 onto this shaft. It should turn freely. Place a ⅛" spacer, with a ¹⁷⁄₆₄" hole, onto the shaft in front of the assembly.

Step 12: Finish assembly. Finally, glue the spinner with the ¼" hole on the tip of the top shaft.

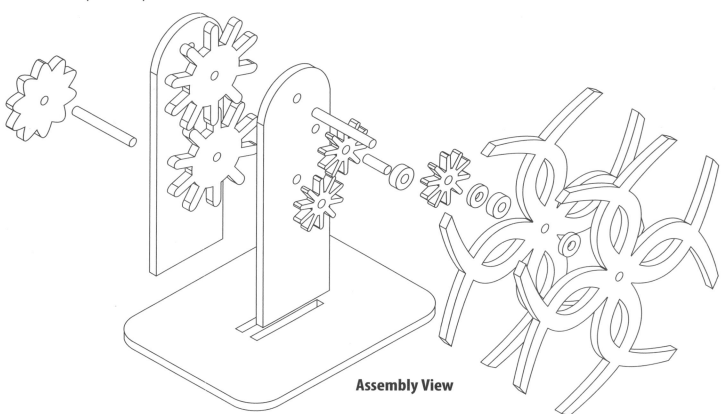

Assembly View

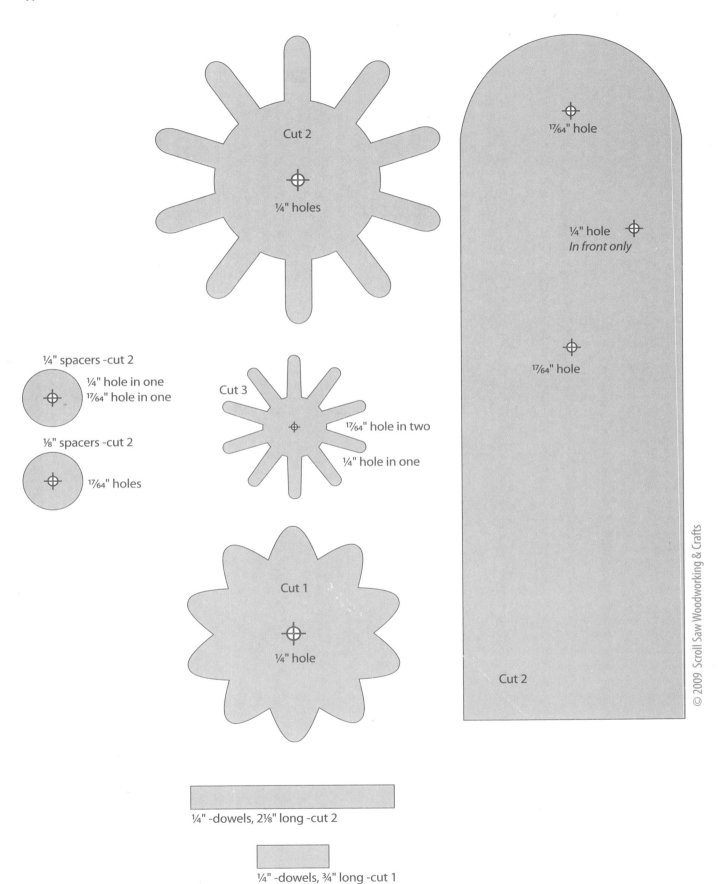

Cut 2

¼" holes

¼" spacers -cut 2

¼" hole in one
¹⁷⁄₆₄" hole in one

⅛" spacers -cut 2

¹⁷⁄₆₄" holes

Cut 3

¹⁷⁄₆₄" hole in two

¼" hole in one

Cut 1

¼" hole

¹⁷⁄₆₄" hole

¼" hole
In front only

¹⁷⁄₆₄" hole

Cut 2

¼" -dowels, 2⅛" long -cut 2

¼" -dowels, ¾" long -cut 1

Base

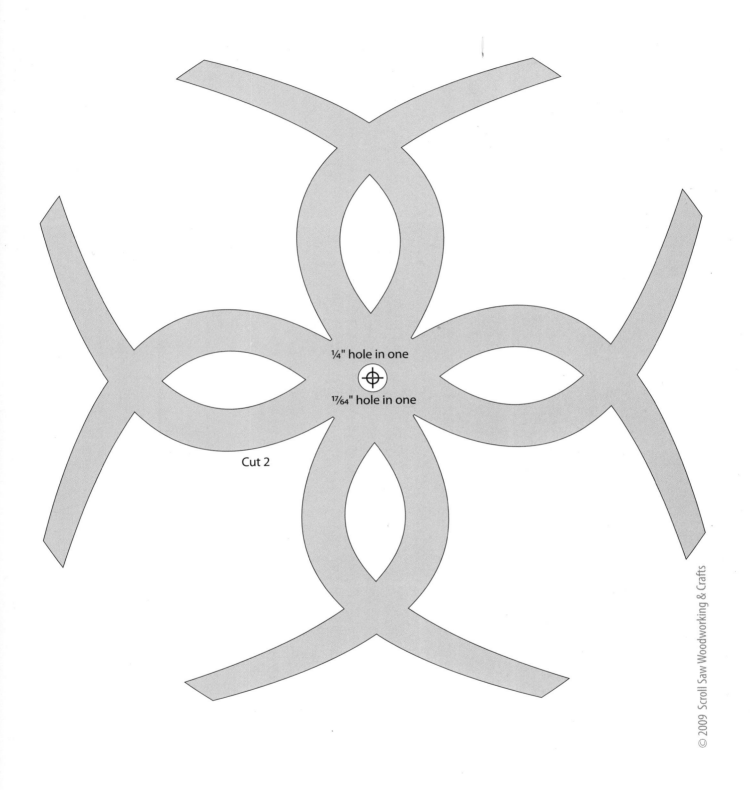

¼" hole in one

¹⁷⁄₆₄" hole in one

Cut 2

Inlay and Relief

Inlay projects involve cutting and placing one piece of contrasting wood inside another. Although inlay is often done with veneer, you can use some hardwoods to inlay on the scroll saw. In relief projects, as the name suggests, parts protrude out from the surface of the carving. Relief cutting can produce parts that recess as well. To achieve inlay or relief on a scroll saw, you'll need a saw that tilts right and left. Which way and how much the saw tilts helps determine whether the wood protrudes or recesses in relief pieces.

Inlay Earrings

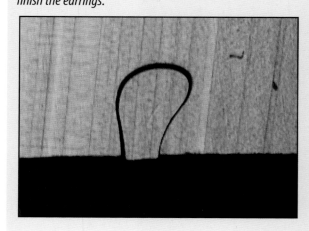

A great project to practice your inlay skills and use up your scrap wood

By Theresa Ekdom

These inlay earrings are an ideal way to use up the scraps of hardwood left after cutting your Christmas ornaments. You can cut several in a day as gifts for family, friends, or yourself!

Stack two contrasting colors of hardwood together by running a bead of hot glue around the outside edges. Do not use double-sided tape; the pieces need to fit tightly together for the inlay to work properly.

Attach the pattern to the work piece and drill blade entry holes for the inlay section with a #63 drill bit. Drill the holes for the earring hooks with a ¹⁄₁₆"-diameter bit.

TEST YOUR INLAY CUTS **TIP**

Tilt your saw table 3½° to the left. Using a #3 blade, cut a circular shape clockwise in the waste area. The top wood will drop into the bottom wood. (Tilting the saw to the right causes the opposite effect). When you separate the two pieces, the contrasting wood should fit flush within the earrings. If the inlay wood is above the contrasting wood, reduce the tilt of the table a little. If the inlay sinks too far into the bottom wood, increase the tilt of the table. Continue experimenting in the waste area until you get a relatively tight fit—minor differences can be sanded out when you finish the earrings.

Cut the inlay

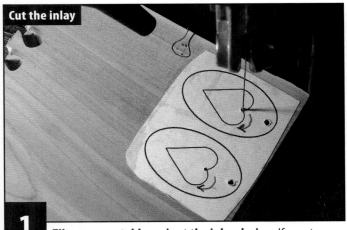

1 **Tilt your saw table and cut the inlay design.** If you stray from the pattern, cut slowly and smoothly back onto the line. To make the sharp turn at the bottom of the heart, hold the wood with your index finger, and gently pull the wood against the back of the blade while swiveling the wood at the same time.

2 **Cut the perimeter of the earring.** Return the table to square, and cut around the perimeter of each earring. You will have one set of inlay earrings, and a set of silhouette heart earrings. Remove the pattern from all of the pieces and separate the layers. Sand the perimeter of the earring to ensure a smooth oval.

Assemble and finish

3 **Assemble and finish the earrings.** Insert the inlay into the earring using white glue. Apply a drop of glue to any hole or line that isn't flush. Sand both sides of the earrings while the glue is wet, reducing the thickness to approximately 1/16". Allow the glue to dry. Dip each earring into tung oil. Let the oil set; then wipe it off with a lint-free cloth following the manufacturer's directions. Place it on a toothpick inserted into an egg carton, and let it dry.

4 **Attach the earring hook.** Using needle-nose pliers, twist the 6mm jump ring open, and feed it through the hole in each earring. Close the jump ring. Then, twist open the 4mm jump ring, and insert the 4mm ring into the 6mm ring. Insert the end of the hooked wire onto the 4mm jump ring, and close the 4mm ring.

Materials & Tools

Materials:
- ¼" x 3" x 3" hardwood of choice, 2 contrasting colors
- Hot-melt glue gun and glue sticks (for stack cutting)
- Glue stick or temporary bond spray adhesive
- White glue
- Sandpaper and sander, 120 grit
- Tung oil and lint-free rag
- 2 each 6mm jump rings (one for each earring)
- 2 each 4mm jump rings (one for each earring)
- 2 each earring hooks (wires, one for each earring)

Tools:
- #3 regular-tooth blades or blades of choice
- Drill with 1/16"-diameter, and #63 drill bits
- Needle-nose pliers

TIP

Earring wires and jump rings can be found in the crafts department of many stores.

Photocopy at 100%

© 2009 Scroll Saw Woodworking & Crafts

Salt and Pepper Shakers

Create attractive inlays without blade entry holes

By Gary MacKay

These durable salt and pepper shakers will look great at your outdoor events. They are a perfect way to show off your skills or to make a thoughtful gift.

The idea for this project started when I was inlaying a dark-colored wood inside a light-colored wood for tree ornaments. No matter what I did to fill it, you could still see the blade entry hole. In the past, I made cuts with the grain, then glued and clamped the saw kerf closed. I proceeded to test cut an inlay, using this technique. It worked great with NO hole to fill in.

The contrasting box-joint trim is made using stack-cutting techniques. Small amounts of expensive woods are ideal for this project.

Cutting

1 **Cut the shaker sides.** Cut four salt and four pepper shaker side patterns. Use spray adhesive to adhere one pattern at a time to the ¼" x 2½" x 17" shaker sides stock. Cut each side. Do not remove the patterns. Separate the salt and pepper shaker sides, and place them pattern-side down.

2 **Cut the box joint trim.** Cut eight ½"-wide walnut and oak trim pieces. Adhere the trim pieces to the shaker sides using double-sided tape. Both shakers should have two sides with walnut and two sides with oak. Cut both pattern lines on the shaker sides. Keep the trim pieces with the sides.

Glue the sides

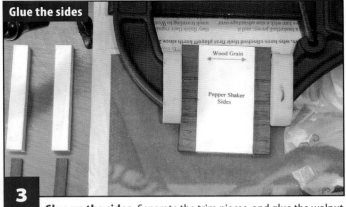

3 **Glue up the sides.** Separate the trim pieces, and glue the walnut and oak to the poplar sides. Keep the pieces in order for a good fit. Use a quick grip clamp to hold the trim pieces to the sides. Wipe off any excess glue, and leave the pieces clamped for 30 minutes. Let dry overnight, then remove the patterns.

Inlay

4 **Inlay the P center.** Align the grain with the arrow on the pattern. Stack the walnut and poplar inlay with poplar on top. With the table tilted (see Make a Test Inlay), cut along the red dashed line. Separate the pieces. Use a pin to place glue into the walnut kerf and circle. Clamp the kerf closed, insert the center of the *P* and let it dry.

5 **Inlay the letters.** Attach the letter patterns using a pin to line up the *P* with the inner circle inlay. On two sides with walnut trim, make a pencil line ⅝" up from the bottom. Line up the bottom of the inlay stock with the lines, and attach them with double-sided tape. With your table tilted, cut the dashed lines.

Assemble and sand

6 **Assemble and sand the sides.** Glue and clamp the kerfs closed, glue in the inlays, and let dry. Make a holding jig by gluing a ⅛"-thick piece to the end of a larger piece of scrap wood. The ⅛" piece acts as a cleat and keeps the wood from sliding. Use a belt sander and the holding jig to sand both surfaces of all the sides.

Make the joints

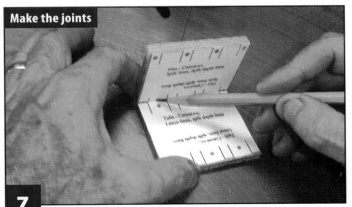

7 **Prepare the box joint cuts.** Practice on scrap wood before cutting the shaker sides. Adhere one pins and one tails pattern to the scrap stock. Lay one side on a flat surface and line the other side up against the edge. Mark the depth with a pencil. Repeat the process to mark all four sides. Square your blade to the saw table.

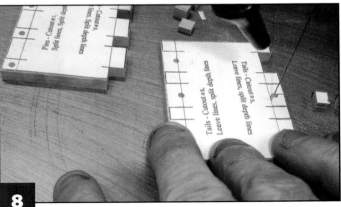

8 **Test-cut the box joints.** Cut up to depth line, cutting to the inside of the pre-printed lines on the tails and splitting the lines on the pins. Cut out the waste, marked with a dot. Cut right on the depth line. Test fit the joints. Mark any sections that bind with a pencil, and shave off the marks with the scroll saw for a good fit.

Assemble the box

9 **Assemble the sides.** Adhere the pins and tails patterns to the sides. Mark the depth lines and cut the box joints. Remove the patterns and test fit the sides. Spread glue into the box joints, and slide the sides together. Clamp the shakers together. After 10 minutes, clean up any glue squeeze-out. Allow to dry overnight.

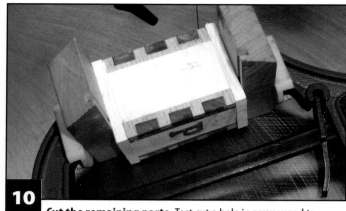

10 **Cut the remaining parts.** Test cut a hole in scrap wood to match your cork. It should protrude less than ¼". Adhere the patterns for the shaker bottoms, drill blade entry holes, and cut the circles to match your cork. Drill and cut the stands and tops. Use a belt sander to level off the top and bottom of the sides. Glue and clamp the tops and bottoms in place and allow to dry.

Finish

11 **Finish the shakers.** Place clear tape over the condiment and cork holes to prevent dust from getting inside. Use a belt sander to sand the sides, and round over all the corners. Glue the stands onto the shaker bottoms. Apply your clear finish of choice.

Materials & Tools

Materials:

- ¼" x 2½" x 17" poplar (shaker sides)
- ¼" x 2½" x 4" walnut (box joint trim)
- ¼" x 2½" x 4" oak (box joint trim)
- 2 pieces ¼" x 1½" x 4" scrap wood (test inlay)
- 2 pieces ¼" x 1¼" x 1¼" walnut (S and P inlays)
- ¼" x 1¼" x 1¼" poplar (P center)
- 2 pieces ¼" x 2" x 2½" scrap wood (test box joints)
- ¼" x 2" x 2" scrap wood (test bottom)
- 4 pieces ¼" x 2" x 2" poplar (shaker tops and bottoms)
- 2 pieces ¼" x 2" x 2" poplar (stands)
- Wood glue

- 2 each ⅝"-diameter corks (available at hardware and craft stores)
- 4 pieces ¾" x 1" x 3" scrap wood (clamping blocks)
- Spray adhesive
- Double-sided tape
- Clear packaging tape
- Assorted grits of sandpaper
- Clear finish of choice

Tools:

- #5 reverse-tooth blade or blades of choice
- Drill with ³⁄₃₂"-diameter bit
- Belt sander
- Awl (to remove glue squeeze-out)
- Pin (to align pattern)
- Toothpick
- 2 quick-grip clamps

MAKE A TEST INLAY **TIP**

Stack the inlay test pieces together with double-sided tape and attach the test pattern. Tilt the right side of your saw table down 3°. Use a #5 blade to cut along the dashed line in a counterclockwise direction, cutting

out the circle. The bottom circle should drop out. Separate the pieces, and clamp the bottom piece's kerf closed. Test fit the top circle into the bottom piece. If the circle fits tightly (not flush), then reset the table to 2½° and re-test. If the circle fits too loosely, then reset the table to 3½°, and re-test. I use the 3° table tilt.

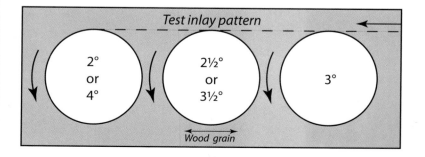

Test inlay pattern

| 2° or 4° | 2½° or 3½° | 3° |

Wood grain

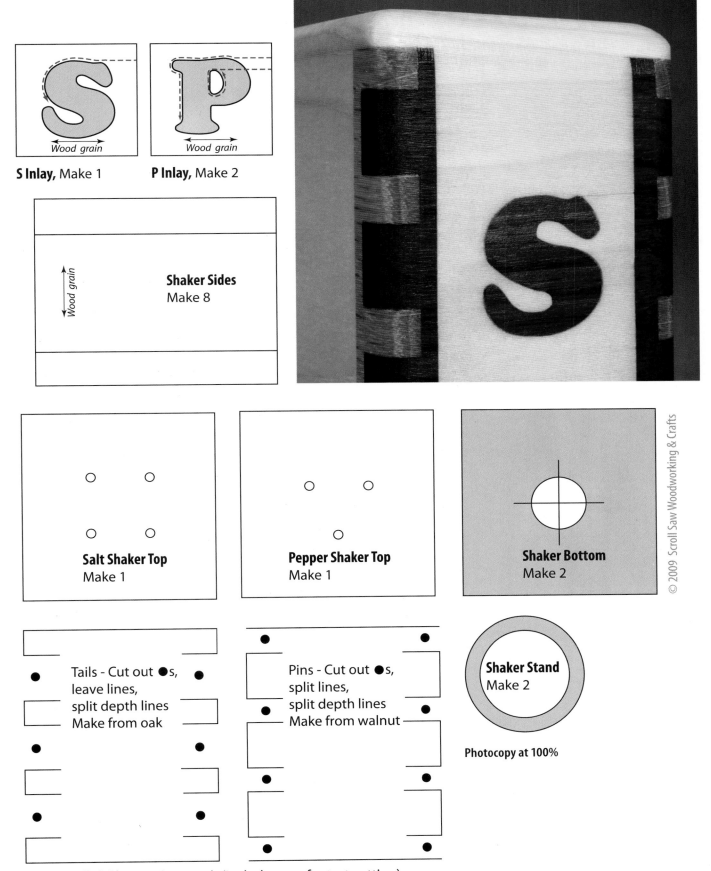

S Inlay, Make 1

P Inlay, Make 2

Wood grain

Wood grain

Shaker Sides
Make 8

Wood grain

Salt Shaker Top
Make 1

Pepper Shaker Top
Make 1

Shaker Bottom
Make 2

Shaker Stand
Make 2

Photocopy at 100%

Tails - Cut out ●s,
leave lines,
split depth lines
Make from oak

Pins - Cut out ●s,
split lines,
split depth lines
Make from walnut

Tails & Pins - Make 5 each (includes one for test cutting)

© 2009 Scroll Saw Woodworking & Crafts

Relief Cutting Secrets
Tilt your tabletop for cool effects

By Rick Hutcheson   Photography by Hetherington Photography

Marylin Carmin's "Hannah Grace," an angel of beauty, shows how relief cutting, fretwork, and veining can be combined for a spectacular presentation. (This image is from the book *Scroll Saw Relief* by Marilyn Carmin.)

A nice addition, technique-wise, to your scrolling arsenal is relief cutting. With relief cuts, you create raised and recessed areas by tilting the tabletop. I'll cover the factors affecting the amount of pop out (raise) or pop in (recess) as well as offer some advice for perfecting your relief cutting technique. As you'll see, because of four interrelated factors, trial and error is the only way to ensure that you end up with the effect you want once you put blade to wood. A practice pattern is included. Make several copies and experiment. It's the best way to learn.

The Basics

Let's begin by reviewing the basics of relief cutting. Relief means that parts of the work piece either raise or recess. Unlike other types of cutting in which you have a cutout plus the waste area, in relief cutting both parts are used. What would be considered the waste is referred to in relief cutting as the "frame."

Which effect—the pop out or the pop in—you'll achieve depends on the direction of the angle (left or right) and the direction of the cut (clockwise or counterclockwise). The accompanying chart shows you how these two factors combine for different effects. The amount of tilt, measured in degrees, and the blade also affect the result. The chart nicely summarizes the first two factors.

The last two merit a bit more explanation. I'll begin with the degree of tilt. Almost all saws have a protractor scale, but how accurate is it? The scale will get you close, but you will still need to fine-tune to get accurate bevels. Using protractors and wedges may help in setting up the bevel you want, but your best bet is to do actual cutting and take measurements from the wood. Always keep in mind that the bevel on the wood is the most important thing. What the protractor reads is not really relevant.

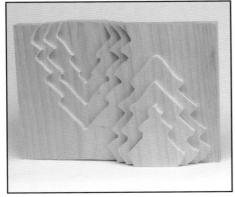

By changing the direction of your cut, you can create either a pop-out effect (right) or a pop-in (left) effect.

Now, let's take a look at the blade. Why does the blade play a part in making relief effects? It has to do with the kerf. The wider the kerf, the more pronounced the effect. The physical blade size obviously affects the kerf. Another factor to consider is the newness of the blade. As the blade's burrs wear off, the kerf narrows. This change in width can be measured in thousandths of an inch, yet it's enough of a change to alter the amount of relief. Take a look at the photo below with the two shapes cut out. The clover was cut with a narrow-kerf blade while the star was cut out with a blade with a wider kerf.

The Finer Points of Relief Cutting

Look at the photo again. Did you notice that there's no cut line coming from the outside edge to the interior? Getting the blade to the inside cutting lines was achieved by drilling a blade entry hole in line with the angle of the table to the blade. Think about how the piece is dropping into the frame, so some of the bevel on the inside bevel of the frame will be showing. Make sure your blade entry hole does not go in this area.

As you cut, your own work habits can affect what happens when the blade is put to wood. When we tilt the table and apply pressure to hold the wood down, we still tend to push straight down, and not at 90° to the angle of the table. Because of this work habit, the wood has a tendency to slide down to the lower side of the table as you cut, making it difficult to cut an accurate bevel. Even though it's a little trickier to make the cut, the sliding doesn't really affect the bevel unless, of course, you get excessive with it.

You'll get the best results if you are consistent throughout the cut. To achieve consistency, I typically slow down the feed rate about every ½" of cut. I simultaneously release the

If the cut out is to inset into the frame, the pilot hole should be drilled into the cut out, as you can see here. The hole should be small enough that it won't be noticeable.

In this example, the star will pop out of the frame. The blade entry hole, therefore, should be positioned on the frame side of the cut line.

BEGINNER BASICS: **TIP**

What's a kerf? What's a bevel?
The kerf is the space that is created after the blade has cut through the wood. The bevel refers to the edge profile of the wood.

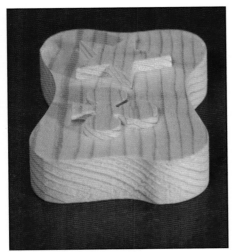

The table angle was not changed to make these two cuts. The difference? The kerf width. The star was cut out with a #7 reverse-tooth blade that has a wider kerf than the #5 reverse-tooth used to cut out the cloverleaf.

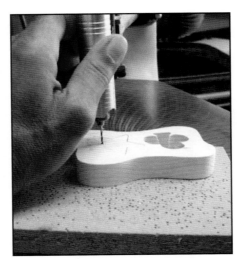

To make a blade entry hole, position the wood so that it is oriented the way it will be cut. Next, align the drill with the blade and make the hole. (I use a moto tool to make the blade entry holes; I find it easier to maneuver.)

CHECKING THE SQUARE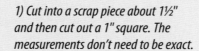

"Squaring the table" means you're adjusting the table tilt so the blade is positioned at a 90° angle to the table surface. To check if it's square, you can use a small machinist square, a sometimes very expensive, but very precise, square. You could also use a business card as a way to check the square. Yet another method is to cut into a block of wood, then pull the block back and reposition to the backside of the blade to see if the cut line is parallel to the blade.

Using these methods, you may adjust your table "to square." The problem is, it may not be square after all! Your best bet is to employ what I call the "cut-square" method using the blade and material you are going to use to make your project. Just follow these simple steps:

1) Cut into a scrap piece about 1½" and then cut out a 1" square. The measurements don't need to be exact.

2) Back out of the cut with the blade.

3) Remove the square block from the wood. Slide it out at the top and out at the bottom. If it slides out in both directions the same, then the table is squared to the blade-cutting path. That doesn't mean it is especially squared to the table, but we are assured that the blade is cutting square on the wood. If your saw has table stops, adjust them now, so that after tilting the table, you can get it back to square easily. As you continue to cut, perform this simple check every so often to assure that your table is always square. Adjust your table as necessary.

Notice that the blade does not line up with either the cut line on the wood or the business card. It would appear that the table is not square.

Keeping exactly the same table setting used in the first photo, I used the "cut-square" method. The block drops out of the bottom and lifts out of the top. The only gap created is from the saw kerf.

Even though the table angle is exactly the same as in the first photo, according to the angle measuring tool, the cut I just made confirms that the table is positioned so the resulting cut is square.

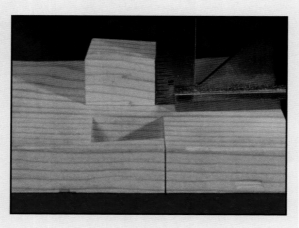

downward pressure just enough to allow the wood to move. Doing so allows the wood to be pulled back by the side of the blade. This technique works because the blade is under tension, which causes the blade to bow to the side. But when the side pressure is released, the blade straightens itself back out, pulling the wood back to center in the process.

Virtually all scroll saw books instruct you to make "angle testers" because of the interplay of the four components that affect how far a cutout pops in or out. In review, they are the direction of the tilt, the direction of the cut, the amount of tilt, and the blade. Experiment, make notes, and master this nifty scroll saw technique. It will add new "dimensions" to your projects.

A MATTER OF DEGREE

The angle of the table tilt determines how far the wood pushes through before it locks into place. The greater the angle, the less it protrudes. Just remember that if you cut a piece out when the table is square (0 degrees), the cutout goes all the way through the wood. So that means as you increase the angle, it has to decrease the distance it protrudes through the wood.

By John A. Nelson

This practice exercise will help you see the magic of relief cutting in action. Basic cutting instructions are included, but the point of having this simple pattern is to allow you to play around with different angles, tilts, and directions of cuts. Make sure you make plenty of copies!

Step 1: *Make a copy of the tree pattern and attach it to the wood with temporary bond spray adhesive.*

Step 2: *Set your saw table at 3°, left side down.*

NOTE: If your saw does not tilt to the left, tilt it to the right and make all of the cuts in the direction opposite of the direction indicated in Steps 3 to 5.

Step 3: *Cutting in a counterclockwise direction, make your cut starting at the IN arrow for Cut 1.*

Step 4: *Repeat Step 3, starting your cut at the IN arrow for Cut 2.*

Step 5: *Repeat Step 3, starting your cut at the IN arrow for Cut 3.*

Following these instructions, all three trees will push out. To make all three trees push in, start all of your cuts on the left side of the pattern and cut clockwise. Mix it up and start cuts 1 and 3 on the right, and cut 2 on the left. Try other combinations and other degrees of tilt. The best way to get a handle on different effects is to practice, practice, practice!

WHICH EFFECT CHART   **TIP**

Table Angle	Raised Effect	Recessed Effect
Right	Cut Clockwise	Cut Counter-Clockwise
Left	Cut Counter-Clockwise	Cut Clockwise

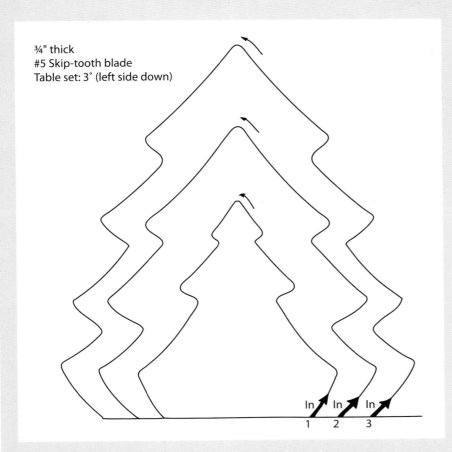

¾" thick
#5 Skip-tooth blade
Table set: 3° (left side down)

In   In   In
1   2   3

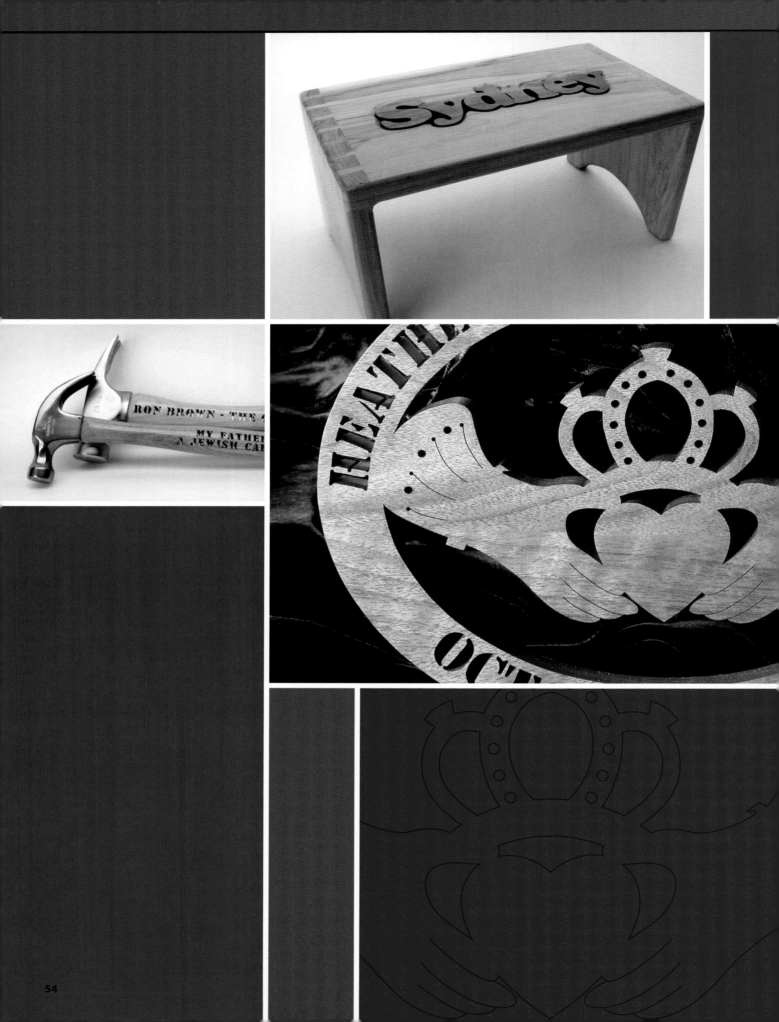

Personalizing

The scroll saw can be a great tool for personalizing projects you have already completed or items you have bought. Following are just a few ideas of what you can do. Use your imagination; the possibilities are limitless.

Personalize It!

Add value to hammers, step stools, desk plaques, and coat racks!

By Ron Brown

A gift to someone with his or her own name actually cut all the way through makes it special. These gifts are unique heirloom treasures to give to friends, coworkers, and relatives. And, if you're doing the craft show circuit, you'll be pleased with how truly quick and easy these personalized gifts are to make.

On the following pages, I'll show you how to create a cool hammer using a nontraditional scrolling technique. Also, using more conventional techniques, I'll show you how to incorporate highly popular name puzzles into three different uses: a child's step stool, a desk plaque, and a coat rack.

A Very Cool Hammer

Step 1: Use a computer and word processor to create your pattern. Select a font named "Stencil." If your word processing program doesn't have it, you'll need to get on the Internet. I found it by searching "stencil +truetype +font" in *www.yahoo.com*. (When you type into search, do not include the quotation marks; all other symbols must be included.) I use a PC, so I clicked on *www.pcworld.com*. The complete, specific URL for the Stencil font I used on my PC is *http://www.pcworld.com/downloads/file_description/0,fid,2518,00.asp*

If you use a Macintosh, you may need to do a little searching to find a download that works for you.

Step 2: Choose a font size that is 30 points or larger. The most common size used for standard hammers with one line is 48 points. Use 30 to 36 points for two lines. Use 54 to 72 points for framing hammers.

Step 3: Spread out the letters. Increase the character spacing by four to eight points or they will be too close and fragile.

Step 4: Apply "Outline" to your font so the letters will print hollow. The outline gives you a very fine line to follow.

Step 5: Prepare the pattern. Cut out the pattern and attach it to the hammer handle. I use temporary bond spray adhesive.

Step 6: Make starter holes. Hammer handles are round, so make starter holes for drilling. Otherwise, the drill point will skid away, and drilling will not be accurate. Use an awl or similar punch to make starting points in each element of each letter. In the Stencil font, there are four elements to cut in the letter *E*.

Step 7: Secure the hammer. If you are using a jig to hold the hammer, mount the hammer before you drill. If you are using an auxiliary table on your scroll saw, you'll also need one for your drill press. (An auxiliary table that is ½" thick x 18" deep x 30" wide eliminates the need for a jig.)

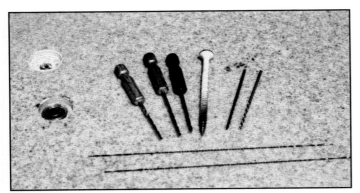

Step 8: Drill the blade entry holes. In the Step 8 photo, three hex shank bits are to the left of the white sheet rock screw. (I use the screw as a punch awl.) To the right of the screw are two regular ⅛" drill bits. Two spiral blades lie below the bits and screws. Use a ¹⁄₁₆" hex shank drill bit. Drill the blade entry holes all the way through the handle. Important: Don't try to drill all of the way through in one stroke. Stop often and clear the chips. Also, use a fairly slow speed. I use 850 rpm.

Step 9: Cut the letters. Install a #0 spiral blade and prepare to cut the letters. If you are using a jig, you will have a lot of mass to move around, so go slowly. For small fonts (30 to 36 points), use a #2/0 spiral. For large fonts (72 points and above), use a #2 spiral. Thread the blade through the first entry hole and turn the speed down to about one half speed—approximately 900 strokes per minute (SPM). Blades last much longer, and it is much easier to follow the patterns.

Step 10: Sand. After the letters are cut, the back of the hammer will have some tear-out. Sand it smooth. Begin with 80- or 100-grit sandpaper, move to 150, and finish with 220. To remove identifying labels that are present on most hammers, use a razor blade and mineral spirits. Sand the entire handle smooth. Start with 100 grit and finish with 220. You'll remove most of the factory finish.

Step 11: Finish with lacquer. Use a spray lacquer to finish the hammer. Apply six coats to the handle and one coat to the hammer's head. You may have to sand lightly between the fifth and sixth coats. Once the final coat dries thoroughly, sign and date the back of the hammer with a fine-point permanent marker.

Making a Jig

If you think "Irish dance" when you hear the word jig, you need to read this section. A jig is a device that enhances the capabilities of your woodworking tools. It allows you to do an operation more safely or more accurately than if you did not use the jig. Follow these steps to make the holding jig for a hammer.

Step 1: Use ½" high-grade plywood. I prefer Baltic birch. Lay out the item (a hammer in this example) on the board. The sled or base should be approximately 6" longer than the item because you need 3" on either end for the clamps.

Step 2: Make the jig body. Trace an area under the handle to be removed, leaving the last ½" to support the very end of the handle. You will need this area for blade clearance. Cut this section with a regular #7 scroll saw blade. As you position the hammer for tracing, keep in mind that it usually touches in only three places when lying flat on a table. The three contact points are the edge of the striking head, the tip of the claw, and the tip of the hammer handle. The hammer doesn't have to be perfectly level, but it does need to be held in one position (relative to the jig base) during drilling and the cutting of the handle. You may add a couple of stops around the steel head if you wish, but they are not necessary. To add stops, obtain some ¼" x 4" carriage bolts, matching wing nuts, and washers.

Step 3: Make a V block to hold the end of the handle. Cut a slot in the middle to make it adjustable.

Step 4: Make two "whistle"-style cam clamps. They'll have slots cut lengthwise in the middle, which will provide bolt clearance with leverage to hold the object down when the wing nuts are tightened.

These jig-making techniques can also be used on many other projects up to about 1½" thick. I have used these techniques to cut pool cues, full-size baseball bats, mini bats, sheet rock saws, Ping Pong paddles, ¾" flat boards, and coping saw handles.

Step Stool Name Puzzle

I wanted to make something special for my grandchildren, and it had to last a lifetime. I came up with a really cool dovetailed step stool that has their first names cut out in the middle. Each letter is really a puzzle piece and, even at three years old, the grandkids put those puzzles together amazingly fast. This step stool puzzle makes a great present, and even if you use top-grade hardwood, you won't spend more than $10 on material.

Step 1: Make the pattern. I use my computer and choose the "CopperBlk" font in outline mode at around 220 points. I also condense the spacing between the letters by several points. I want the letters to overlap each other (see the photos throughout this project).

Step 2: Drill. With the pattern adhered to your work piece, drill the blade entry holes for the inside cuts. You can use just about any size bit. Next, drill a hole in the waste so you can cut out the first letter. The cuts will be made on the outside of the letters, so the position of the starting hole isn't all that important. Just make sure the hole won't be noticeable in the finished product.

Step 3: Make all inside cuts first. I like to use a #7 reverse-tooth blade, but use the blade you prefer.

Step 4: Cut out the letters. Cut out the first letter completely, remove it, and do the other letters. Completely cut out each letter so they are finished products.

Step 5: Clean up the silhouette left by the letters. With all letters removed, clean up the silhouette by removing the long skinny pieces, which will easily break off during use.

Step 6: Round the silhouette. Use a ¼" round-over bit to ease the edges of the silhouette only! Do not attempt to round over the letters themselves unless you are working with letters over three inches tall.

Step 7: Cut the dovetails to attach the legs. Drill the screw holes, if you are not using dovetails.

Step 8: Assemble the stool.

Step 9: Add a ⅛" or ¼" backer. Attach it to the underside of the stool so the letters won't fall through.

Step 10: Apply the finish. Oil works fine as does polyurethane and lacquer.

GETTING IN THE SMALL SPACES   TIP

For small spaces, I like to use a very inexpensive steel round-over router bit with a very narrow guide pin, the kind Sears sells for about $10. Either ⅛" or ¼" radius works fine. The very small pilot guide on the end of this bit enables you to get into very tight spaces, such as the ones you encounter when you cut these kinds of puzzles. If you have a variable speed router or a speed controller, use the slowest speed setting to avoid burning the wood.

Desk Plaque Puzzles

The plaque is made almost exactly the same way as the stool. It is approximately 3" high x 16" long and made of two pieces of ¾"-thick material.

Step 1: Create the pattern. To get the pattern, follow the same procedure as described in Step 1 in the Step Stool Name Puzzle section. Cut out the name centered in one piece of wood and round over the silhouette as described in Step 6 of the same section.

Step 2: Put it all together. Glue the second piece of wood to the back of the first. Don't get glue on the silhouette or the glue will show. You now have a block of wood that is 1½" thick. True up the top, bottom, and ends by sanding, using a router with a flush trim bit, a jointer or planer, or whatever tool you have that will work. The back piece you just glued on will act as a stop to keep the letters from falling through.

Name Plaque Coat Racks

Follow the same procedures that are used for making the step stools and name plaque puzzles, but start out with bigger wood. Because the letters will be much taller (read: easier to cut out), you'll need to start with a blank at least ¾" x 6" x 12" wide. A larger piece would be even better, say 9" x 16". No backing is needed on these items because they will be hung against the wall. I use shaker pegs for the coat hooks, but you could use metal coat hooks. I use a keyhole cutter router bit to make the vertical slots on the back of the items. I begin the cut in the open section of the silhouette, stopping about 1" from the top. I make one cut on the left and the other on the right.

Materials & Tools

Materials:
- Hammer with wooden handle
- ¾" up to 1½" oak or maple in size large enough to accommodate selected name (Step Stool, Desk Plaque, Coat Rack projects)
- Temporary bond spray adhesive
- Sandpaper, 80 or 100, 150, 220 grits
- Mineral spirits
- Gloss spray lacquer
- Fine-point permanent marking pen

Tools:
- Awl
- Drill with ¹⁄₁₆" hex shank bit (Hammer project)
- #2/0, #0, #2 spiral blades (Hammer project)
- #7 reverse-tooth blade (Step Stool project)
- Razor blade
- Router with ¼" round-over bit (Step Stool project)

Celtic Anniversary Claddagh

Add another chapter to your anniversary memories

By Rick Hutheson

Design by Chuck Bookbinder

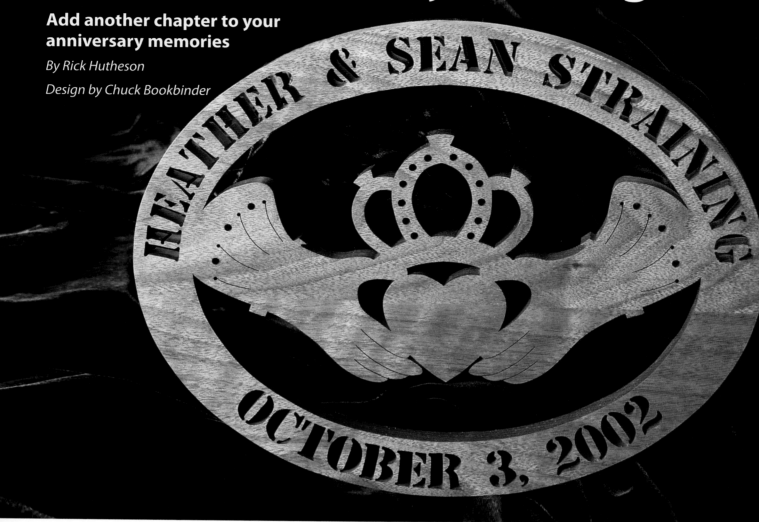

Here's a project that can turn the day into a romantic one for you and your significant other. Present him or her with a token of your affection: a wooden wedding anniversary plaque that has the look of a claddagh ring.

Be sure the coast is clear when you're working on this project and that you've got a good hiding place to put it. Then, you'll be able to enjoy your spouse's surprised look when you hand over the finished plaque.

Step 1: Prepare the wood. Using 180-grit sandpaper, finish sand the wood before applying the pattern. Sanding the wood now is easier than sanding the delicate parts after the cutting has been completed.

Step 2: Attach the pattern. Apply the claddagh pattern to the board with temporary bond spray adhesive.

Materials & Tools

Materials:
- ½" x 12" x 9" walnut
- Temporary bond spray adhesive
- Woodworker's glue
- Gloss clear wood finish
- Sandpaper, 180 and 220 grit
- Tack cloth

Tools:
- Table saw
- #2 blade
- Drill with ⅛"- and 1⁄16"-diameter bits

Step 3: Drill the blade entry holes. They're needed in the glove and crown. Use a ⅛" bit. The glove holes on the line ends should be drilled with a 1⁄16" bit. I like using a moto-tool to drill the small starting holes because it is easier than trying to move the wood around on the drill press.

Step 4: Make the inside cuts. Use a #2 blade. I normally cut the smallest areas first, leaving the larger areas to add support. Be careful where you grab the wood as you are making cuts. There are many delicate parts that could be broken. I try to hold the wood with my fingers on the outside edges of the board so I don't break the delicate parts.

Step 5: Cut the letters, numbers, and comma. Be sure you have an entry hole for each piece of the letters and numbers and one for the comma. It's crucial that the letters and numbers look as identical as possible so take occasional breaks during this part of the project. Cut the outside of the plaque after all of the inside fret cuts are completed.

Step 6: Finish sand the project with 220-grit sandpaper. The insides of the cutouts do not need to be sanded because the blade leaves these surfaces smooth.

Step 7: Finish the piece. Wipe the wood with a tack cloth to remove any dust. I finished this piece with two coats of gloss clear wood finish. I prefer to use the spray version.

GLUING BOARDS FOR FRETWORK | **TIP**

If the project calls for a 9"-wide board and you don't have one that wide, you can make one by putting two smaller boards together. For fretwork projects, make sure you edge glue two narrower boards rather than joining them with dowels or biscuits, which would be visible after you make the fret cuts.

THE LEGEND OF CLADDAGH | **TIP**

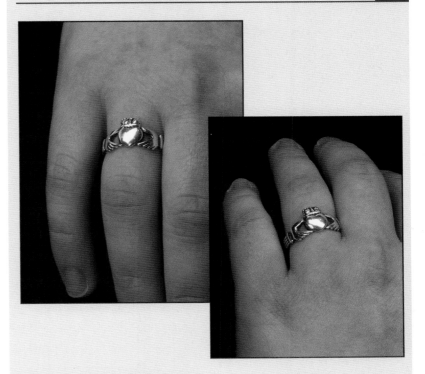

It's easy to enhance a piece like this one as a gift or for sale by including an account of the legend, origin, or special meaning behind the project. Try experimenting with different types or colors of paper. With this addition, you will not only educate the gift recipient or customer but also add value by highlighting the item's special qualities. And don't forget to sign your work.

This particular legend takes place in the village of Claddagh in Galway, Ireland, around the sixteenth century. One morning, a boat went out to sea and was captured by pirates, and the crew was taken as slaves. One man of the crew, who was to have been married within the week, now had no hope of seeing his true love again. The pirates eventually sold the man to a wealthy Moorish gold-smith, under whose rule the man became a master goldsmith. Still remembering his lost love, the man created a ring for her. The elements of the design each had its own meaning—the

heart symbolizing love, the hands holding the heart symbolizing friendship, and the crown symbolizing loyalty. After many long years of slavery, the man finally returned to his village, looking for his true love. To his overwhelming happiness, he not only found her, but also found that she had never married. The man gave her the ring, the two were soon married, and they were never parted again.

Today, the claddagh ring has gained much popularity, still representing love, friendship, and loyalty. The ring has even more significance depending on the way it is worn. If you wear it on your right hand with the crown facing inward, it means that your heart has not yet been claimed. If you wear it on your right hand with the crown facing outward, you hold a special commitment to someone. If you wear it on your left hand, with the crown facing outward, you and your love have been united forever.

Photocopy at 150%

Eagle Mini Desk Clock

A perfect project for inexpensive 1⅜" clock inserts— plus bonus patterns for elk, coyote, and pheasant clocks

By Rick and Karen Longabaugh
Cut by Ernie Lang

Clocks are a perennial favorite for scrollers. This silhouette clock pattern from The Berry Basket is sure to please crafters and collectors alike. Because the fretwork insert is interchangeable, it's easy to design other silhouettes to customize these clocks for customers or as personalized gifts.

We've also included insert patterns for elk, pheasant, and coyote—make a set of four or choose your favorite.

The eagle clock is a classic project to celebrate a person's ability to soar.

Step 1: Sand the pieces. Start with 100-grit sandpaper. Continue to sand with progressively finer sandpaper up to 220 grit.

Step 2: Copy the patterns. Attach them to your wood of choice with temporary bond spray adhesive. The pattern will be easier to remove if you apply the adhesive to the back of the paper rather than to the wood.

Step 3: Drill blade entry holes for all the interior cuts. Use a drill press if you have one to make sure the holes are square.

Step 4: Cut out the silhouette. Use the #3 blade and start in the innermost section. Work your way from the center out.

Step 5: Carefully cut the veins for the eagle's feathers and body detail. Use the #3 blade to cut along the line, then back the blade out.

Step 6: Cut the outside profile. Use the #7 blade. Or, because the outer frame needs to be square to fit into the clock frame, cut the border on a table saw.

Step 7: Drill the 1⅜" hole for the clock insert. Use a Forstner bit. Alternately, you can cut the hole for the clock insert with the scroll saw, but you may need to sand the hole a little for the insert to fit properly.

Step 8: Cut out the frame, top, and base. If you have a table saw, it is easier to make the long, straight cuts. But you can make the cuts on the scroll saw using a large blade (#7 or #9); you'll just need to straighten up the edges by sanding.

Step 9: Cut the hole for the fretwork insert in the frame. Drill blade entry holes near a side and cut it out using a large blade. When finished, round the edges over with a router and a ¼"-diameter round-over bit. Then, round over the edges of the top, frame, and base using the same router bit.

MAKING CLOCK WITHOUT A RABBET TIP

Test cutter Ernest Lang suggests you use a ½"-thick piece and a ¼"-thick piece for the clock body. Cut the hole for the fretwork insert in the ¼"-thick piece (to take the place of the ¼"-deep rabbet). Then, cut a hole ¼" smaller in the ½"-thick piece to frame the fretwork insert and hold it in place. Glue them together to get the ¾"-thick piece without needing to cut a rabbet or clean a rabbet's corners.

Step 10: Cut the ¼"-wide x ¼"-deep rabbet for the eagle insert. (See the pattern.) The easiest way to cut the rabbet is to use a router and rabbet bit. Set the router to cut ¼" deep and use a router fence to cut a ¼"-wide rabbet. Use a chisel to clean out the corners so the insert will fit tightly. Alternatively, you can cut most of the rabbet by cutting most of the slot out with a table saw. Use a chisel to clean out the corners (see Making Clock Without a Rabbet to avoid this step).

Step 11: Re-sand the pieces lightly. Use 220-grit sandpaper to remove any burrs left behind by the saw blades.

Step 12: Assemble the clock. Glue and clamp the frame together using wood glue. Allow to dry overnight. Then, glue the eagle insert into the frame, clamp, and allow to dry overnight.

Step 13: Finish with an oil finish of your choice. Follow the manufacturer's directions for best results.

Step 14: Spray the completed project with a spray varnish.

Step 15: Add the clock insert. Place it in the clock according to the manufacturer's directions.

Materials & Tools

Materials:
- ¼" x 2½" x 3" hardwood of choice (eagle insert)
- ⅜" x 1" x 3½" hardwood of choice (top and bottom)
- ¾" x 3" x 5" hardwood of choice (clock body)
- 1⅜" clock insert
- Wood glue
- Oil finish of choice
- Spray varnish of choice

Tools:
- #3 reverse-tooth blade
- #7 or #9 reverse-tooth blade
- Several clamps
- Sandpaper, 100, 150, 180, and 220 grits
- 1⅜" Forstner bit
- Table saw or router (to cut rabbet and square up sides)

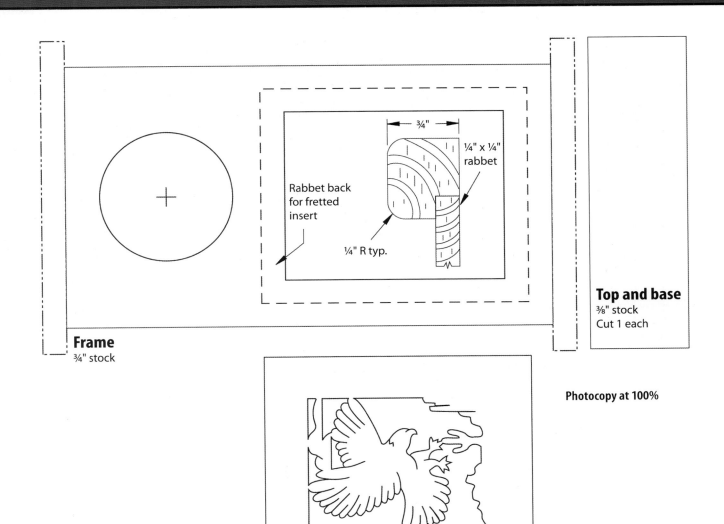

Frame
¾" stock

Rabbet back
for fretted
insert

¾"

¼" x ¼"
rabbet

¼" R typ.

Top and base
⅜" stock
Cut 1 each

Photocopy at 100%

Eagle

Elk

Pheasant

Coyote

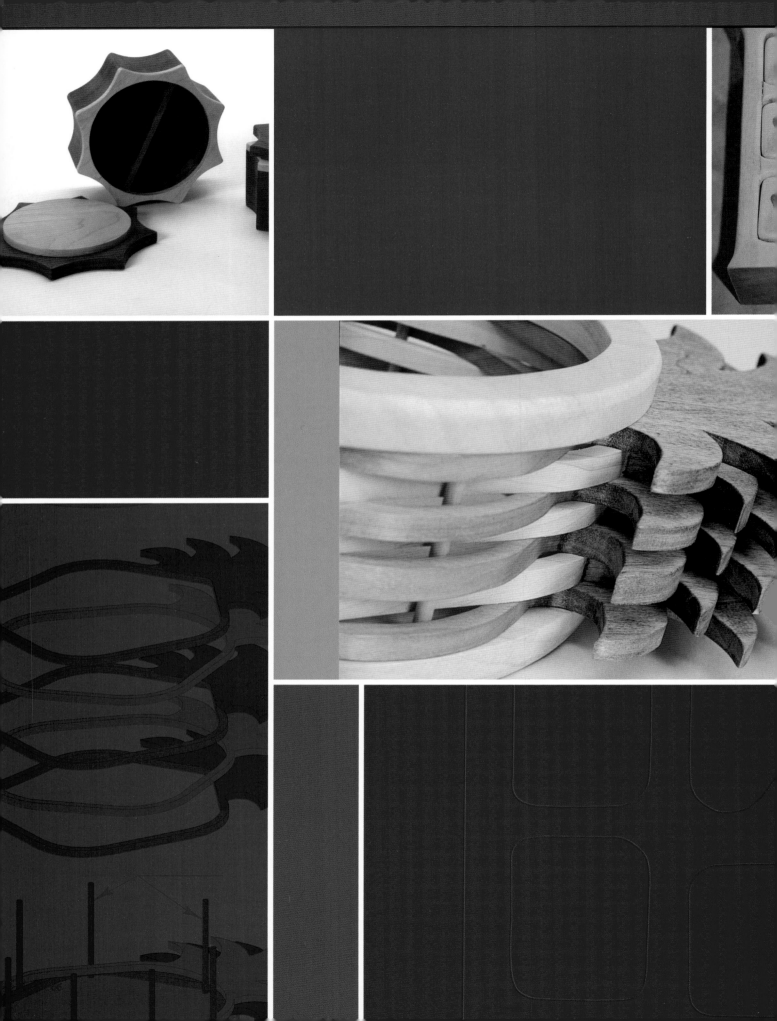

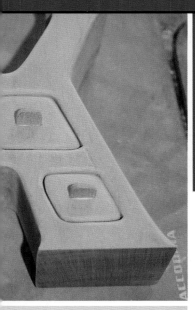

Baskets and Boxes

Though they aren't something you immediately associate with the scroll saw, baskets are popular projects. By cutting and then stacking individual layers, you get a strong but beautiful wooden basket that can be enjoyed for years to come. Like baskets, boxes are popular woodworking projects that can be made on a scroll saw. Some of them can be elegant and simple, while others are more complex. Try the boxes in this section to gain an understanding of the process using a scroll saw. Once you get the hang of it, there are all types of boxes you can make. They are easily customized in terms of the woods you use, the types of drawers and handles you choose, and many more elements.

Pineapple Basket

By Laura Brubaker

This pineapple basket is a very simple scroll saw project with a beautiful outcome. I had the opportunity to watch accomplished scrollsawer Jim Gress of Bowmansville, Pa., go through the step-by-step process of scrolling this basket. Before beginning, note that while this is not a complicated project to scroll, it does involve staining and gluing, which may make it necessary to spread the project out over two or three days.

Pattern Preparation

Photocopy the patterns as indicated to save the originals for future use. You will need to make two copies of Patterns 1 and 2, as well as two copies of the Rim/Base Pattern.

Patterns 1 and 2 will be scrolled on ⅜" stock, while the Rim/Base Pattern will be scrolled on ¾" stock. Because poplar is a very soft wood, Patterns 1 and 2 can be stacked and cut two at a time. You will need four pieces of Pattern 1, three pieces of Pattern 2, and two pieces of the Rim/Base Pattern.

Be sure to examine the wood for knots before beginning to avoid blemishes in your final project. Cut the wood pieces down to approximate size and temporarily glue the patterns to the wood using a spray adhesive.

Sawing

Start this project by cutting the interior layers of the pineapple (Patterns 1 and 2). Stack two pieces of Pattern 1 (⅜" wood) and fasten securely together using masking tape. Using a #5 reverse-tooth scroll saw blade, scroll the outside contour lines of the two pieces simultaneously. Continue by scrolling the interior lines of Pattern 1.

Once you have completed this step, repeat the same procedure for the second double-stacked set of Pattern 1. Then, follow the same steps to stack cut two layers of Pattern 2. You will repeat the procedure one more time to cut the third piece of Pattern 2 by itself (not stacked).

Before cutting the base and rim layers, use an awl (tap slightly) to mark the eight holes on both the base and rim. Next, fasten the base and rim pieces together securely. Scroll the outside contour lines of the base pattern. Next, separate the two pieces and cut the interior lines of *only* the rim pattern.

Once you have completed cutting all of the patterns, remove the temporary patterns from the pieces.

Materials & Tools

Materials:
- Poplar
  (⅜" stock and ¾" stock)
- Green stain
- Provincial stain

Tools:
- #5 reverse-tooth blade
- ³⁄₁₆"-diameter drill bit
- ³⁄₁₆" dowel rod
- Awl
- Clamps
- Temporary bond spray adhesive
- Glue

Staining

Once your interior layers have been cut (Patterns 1 and 2), the leaves of Pattern 1 can be stained. Using a green stain, brush the stain onto the leaves.

Next, stain the body of the pineapple on the same pieces (of Pattern 1), using any type of provincial stain.

Leave the stain on for 8 to 10 minutes and then wipe it off, using a cloth or rag. Allow the stained layers to dry overnight.

Drilling

Using the eight holes that you marked with the awl as your guide, use a ³⁄₁₆"-diameter drill bit to drill about halfway (³⁄₈" deep) through the wood of the base pattern.

Repeat the same procedure as above and drill the holes in your Rim pattern.

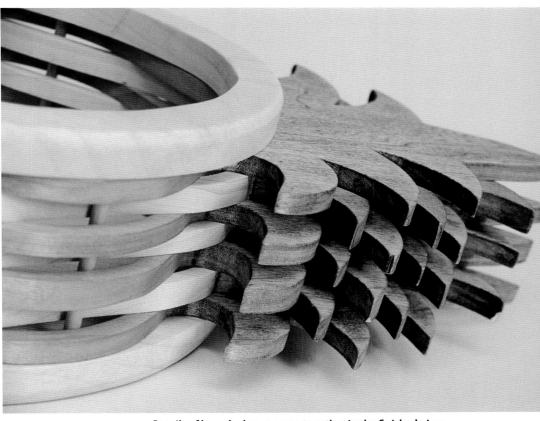

Details of how the layers come together in the finished piece.

Assembling the Basket

Once your stained layers have dried overnight, do a "dry test," by stacking the pieces of the basket together without the dowel rods in place. Once the basket is "assembled," measure the distance between the inside edges of the top and bottom layer. Now add the thickness of the wood for the base and rim layers (about ³⁄₈" because you drilled about halfway through both layers). The final number will be the length that you should cut down your dowel rod. You will need a total of eight dowel rod pieces.

Once you have cut down your eight dowel rod pieces to the same size, place glue in all of the holes of the base. Place the dowel rods in the holes. Now, stack the interior layers of the pineapple, beginning with a stained layer. Next, place glue in the holes of the rim and place the rim on top. Use about five small clamps to clamp the basket together. Once you have clamped the basket, be sure to align the leaves of the interior pineapple layers. Allow the basket to dry overnight.

Other baskets made by Jim Gress.

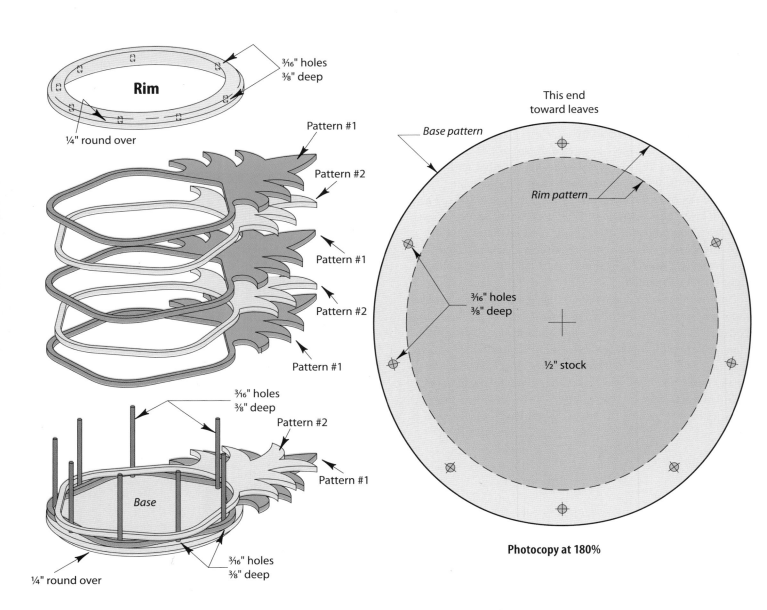

Rim

¾₆" holes
⅜" deep

¼" round over

Pattern #1

Pattern #2

Pattern #1

Pattern #2

Pattern #1

¾₆" holes
⅜" deep

Pattern #2

Pattern #1

Base

¼" round over

¾₆" holes
⅜" deep

This end
toward leaves

Base pattern

Rim pattern

¾₆" holes
⅜" deep

½" stock

Photocopy at 180%

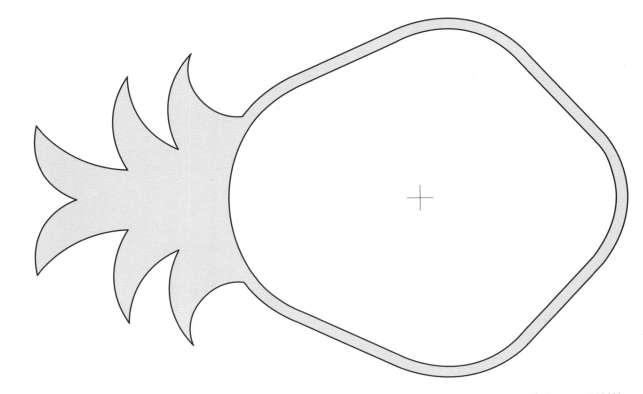

Photocopy at 180%

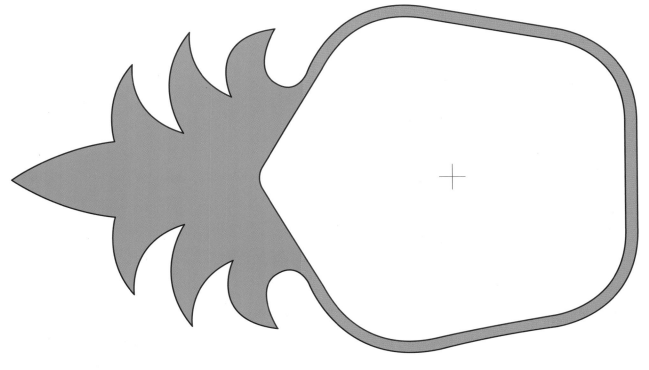

Music Box with Clock

A woven basket with ornate hinges

By John A. Nelson   Scrolled by Bill Guimond

A while back, I came up with an idea that was simple in its concept and execution yet resulted in something really neat. By scrolling out specially patterned "slices," then assembling them together, you could make a wooden basket that looked amazingly like a woven basket. This concept led to several books and articles. I hadn't really thought anything more about the woven basket idea until I discovered oval hinges. Originally, they were designed for ceramic projects. I designed a woven basket pattern around the hinge in order to make use of these unusual hinges. My thanks to Bill Guimond for the great job he did making these music boxes.

Based on feedback received from readers, I slightly altered the assembly process. Lining up the cut slices (or "weaves") proved to be quite a challenge. To ensure quick and easy alignment, I added holes to each weave. Placing dowels in these holes after the cut weaves are assembled guarantees a sure fit.

Step 1: Prepare the wood. To make each piece easier to scroll later, cut your material, allowing ⅛" to ¼" all the way around each of the 14 pieces. Sand the top and bottom surfaces.

Step 2: Make copies of the patterns. Glue them to the wood with temporary bond spray adhesive. Note the quantity of each part; some require one of each, others two of each.

Step 3: Carefully locate and drill all ⅛" holes. For now, drill ⅛" holes where it notes ⁵⁄₃₂" holes. We will redrill them to ⁵⁄₃₂"- diameter holes in Step 9.

Step 4: Carefully cut out all pieces. Use a #2 or #0/2 blade. Sand lightly. Drill the ³⁄₃₂" and ⅜" holes in Weave #3. You want the holes large enough so that the dowel moves freely.

SAVE GLUING TIME WITH SUPER T	TIP

This is one of my favorite glues because it's such a time-saver. It dries in about 30 seconds or less and is perfect for gluing up big projects. You don't need to use clamps or rubber bands to hold the pieces in place. Just glue and go. But, this convenience doesn't come without a price. It is more expensive than conventional glues and it gives off vapors that could send an asthmatic like me to the hospital (I know from experience!). You must use this stuff in a well-ventilated area.

Step 5: Glue the parts. Using two 3" long ⅛" dowels as a temporary guide, glue each part together starting with Weave #1. Glue 1 to 2, 2 to 3, 3 to 4, etc. Do not get the glue near the ⅛" dowel on the right side.

Step 6: Drill. After the glue sets, remove the dowel from the right side. (*See the Assembly View for left/right designations.*) Using a drill press, drill a 5⁄32" diameter hole down to Weave 7. If you don't have a drill press, you can sand the dowel to get the sloppy fit described in Step 4.

Step 7: Glue the dowel. Glue the left ⅛" dowel in place, if necessary.

Step 8: Glue the other dowel. Glue a ¾" long, ⅛" dowel in place on the right side, at the bottom (*see the Assembly View*) through part numbers 1, 2, and 3.

Step 9: Drill. Drill the 5⁄32"-diameter hole down through the ⅛"-diameter hole in the right side. Drill through part numbers 12 through 7 (including part number 7). Why? Refer to the Assembly View and take note of the right side. The large double arrow indicates the position of the dowel that will serve to activate the music movement's on/off mechanism. You want this dowel to fit loosely. Drilling holes for it with the 5⁄32" bit will guarantee what I call a "sloppy" fit. With the extra room, the ⅛" on/off dowel will be able to move freely up and down.

Step 10: Make the plastic window. Drill 3⁄32" holes in the plastic window. Cut out per pattern.

Step 11: Cut the spacer ring. To add the clock insert, first cut the spacer ring.

Step 12: Make the hole for the insert. Carefully, using a Forstner bit, make a 1⅜" hole (or whatever your insert requires) approximately ⅛" deep in the assembly. Take your time here; it's a tricky spot. You want to take care not to cave in the front as you push to drill. Go easy on the pressure. You might also want to shore up the front by placing a shim on the inside.

Step 13: Glue the spacer ring. Using woodworker's glue, secure the spacer ring in place and check to make sure the insert fits correctly.

Step 14: Fit the top lip and lid to the hinge. Make a good snug fit.

Step 15: Rout the lid as shown.

Step 16: Glue the hinge. Using epoxy, glue the hinge to the top lip and lid.

The dowel that activates the on/off lever is seen on the right.

Step 17: Screw the music movement in place. Cut and bend the on/off wire to suit. Bend and cut as per drawing, checking that the on/off wire moves up and down freely.

Step 18: Add the plastic window. Use two small screws or brads.

Step 19: Add a ⅛" on/off dowel. It should be approximately 2⅜" long or to suit. Check that it moves freely up and down and turns the movement on and off when lid opens. To help hold the on/off wire in place, notch the bottom end of the dowel.

Step 20: File the hinge if needed. If necessary, use a metal file to notch the inside of the hinge so that the on/off dowel moves up and down freely.

Step 21: Finish to suit. Add felt pads to the bottom.

HAND-RUBBED FINISHES

I love the look and feel of wood, and for those reasons, I use tung oil or Danish oil. Either one can be applied with your hands. They also soak into the wood instead of adding on to the wood surface like polyurethane. And, rather than sealing the wood's pores, the oils allow the wood to breathe, and, in time, will bring out the natural patina of the wood. One or two coats will leave an attractive, somewhat flat finish. If you prefer a shinier look, you can get that by using either oil. You just need to apply five or six coats.

Top View of Music Movement

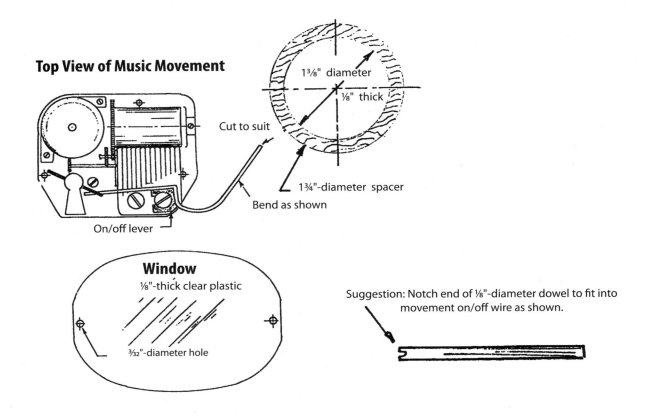

1⅜" diameter

⅛" thick

Cut to suit

1¾"-diameter spacer

Bend as shown

On/off lever

Window
⅛"-thick clear plastic

³⁄₃₂"-diameter hole

Suggestion: Notch end of ⅛"-diameter dowel to fit into movement on/off wire as shown.

Left Side   **Right Side**

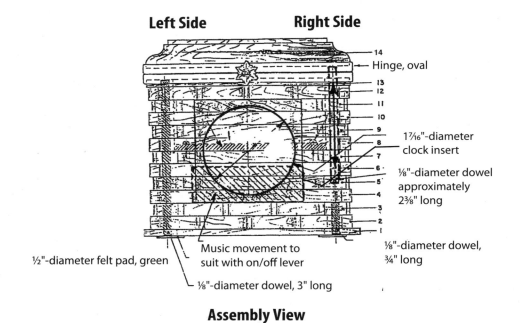

14 — Hinge, oval

13
12
11
10
9
8 — 1⁷⁄₁₆"-diameter clock insert
7
6 — ⅛"-diameter dowel approximately 2⅜" long
5
4
3
2
1

½"-diameter felt pad, green

Music movement to suit with on/off lever

⅛"-diameter dowel, 3" long

⅛"-diameter dowel, ¾" long

Assembly View

Materials & Tools

Materials:

Note: The project seen in this article is made from walnut and aspen. You may choose different woods, but hardwoods work best. Hardwoods include aspen, mahogany, poplar and walnut; cherry is a hardwood but is not recommended because of its tendency to burn in tight turns. Also, choosing contrasting woods—mahogany-walnut, maple-walnut, for example—for the lid and the weaves will yield attractive results.

- 1 piece, ½" x 4½" x 3" (lid)
- 1 piece, ⅛" x 4½" x 3" (top lip)
- 11 pieces, ¼" x 4½" x 3" (weaves)
- 1 piece, ⅛" x 4½" x 3½" (base)
- ⅛" dowels in lengths of 3", 3", 2⅜", and ¾"
- Temporary bond spray adhesive
- Sandpaper, 200 grit (fine)
- Hinges (National Artcraft oval)
- Yellow woodworker's glue
- Epoxy glue
- Music movement
- Clock
- ⅛" x 3½" x 2½" thin plastic (available in stores that sell glass for windows)
- 2, ½" felt pads
- 2, ¼" felt pads
- Finish of choice

Tools:

- Drill with assorted drill bits (⅛", ³⁄₁₆", ⁵⁄₃₂")
- #2 or #0/2 blade
- Forstner bit 1⅜"-diameter (or size recommended by clock insert instructions)

Photocopy at 100%

IMPORTANT: Drill all holes before cutting

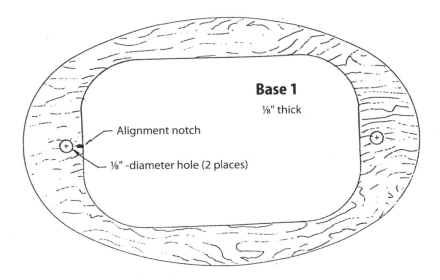

Base 1
⅛" thick

Alignment notch

⅛" -diameter hole (2 places)

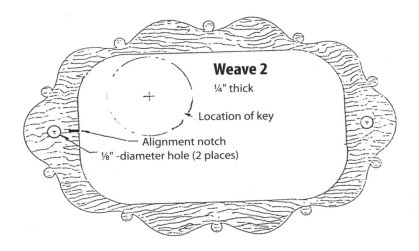

Weave 2
¼" thick

Location of key

Alignment notch

⅛" -diameter hole (2 places)

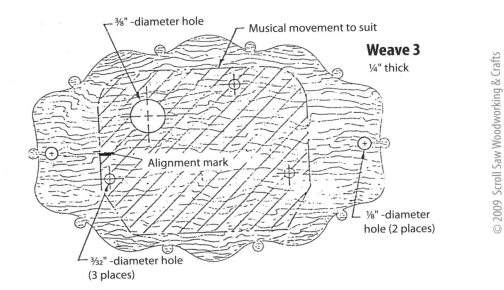

⅜" -diameter hole

Musical movement to suit

Weave 3
¼" thick

Alignment mark

⅛" -diameter hole (2 places)

³⁄₃₂" -diameter hole (3 places)

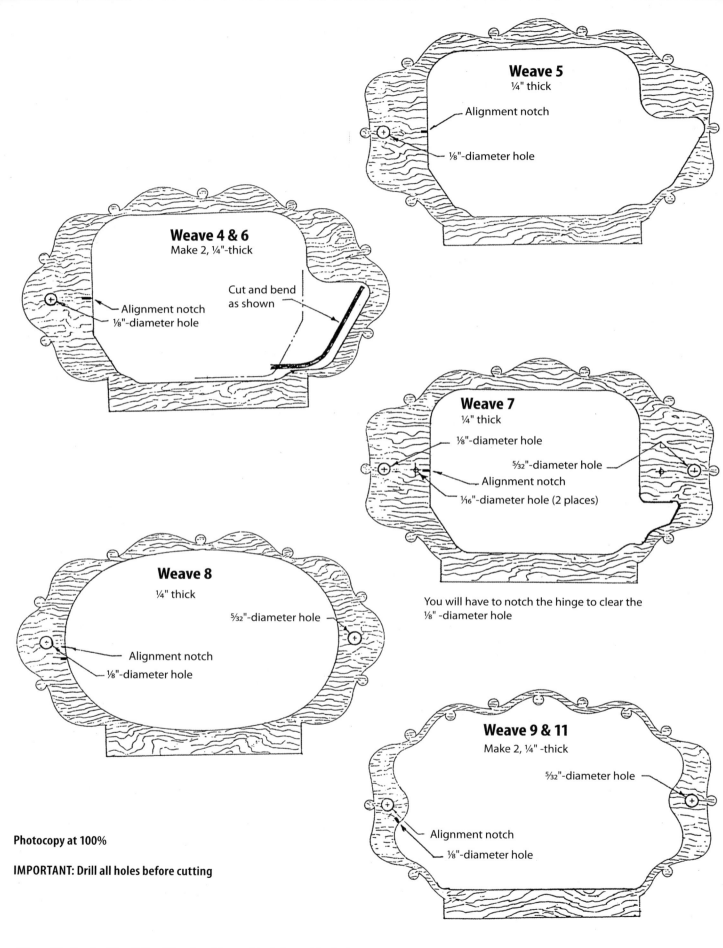

Weave 5
¼" thick

Alignment notch

⅛"-diameter hole

Weave 4 & 6
Make 2, ¼"-thick

Cut and bend
as shown

Alignment notch
⅛"-diameter hole

Weave 7
¼" thick

⅛"-diameter hole

5⁄32"-diameter hole

Alignment notch

1⁄16"-diameter hole (2 places)

You will have to notch the hinge to clear the
⅛"-diameter hole

Weave 8
¼" thick

5⁄32"-diameter hole

Alignment notch

⅛"-diameter hole

Weave 9 & 11
Make 2, ¼"-thick

5⁄32"-diameter hole

Alignment notch

⅛"-diameter hole

Photocopy at 100%

IMPORTANT: Drill all holes before cutting

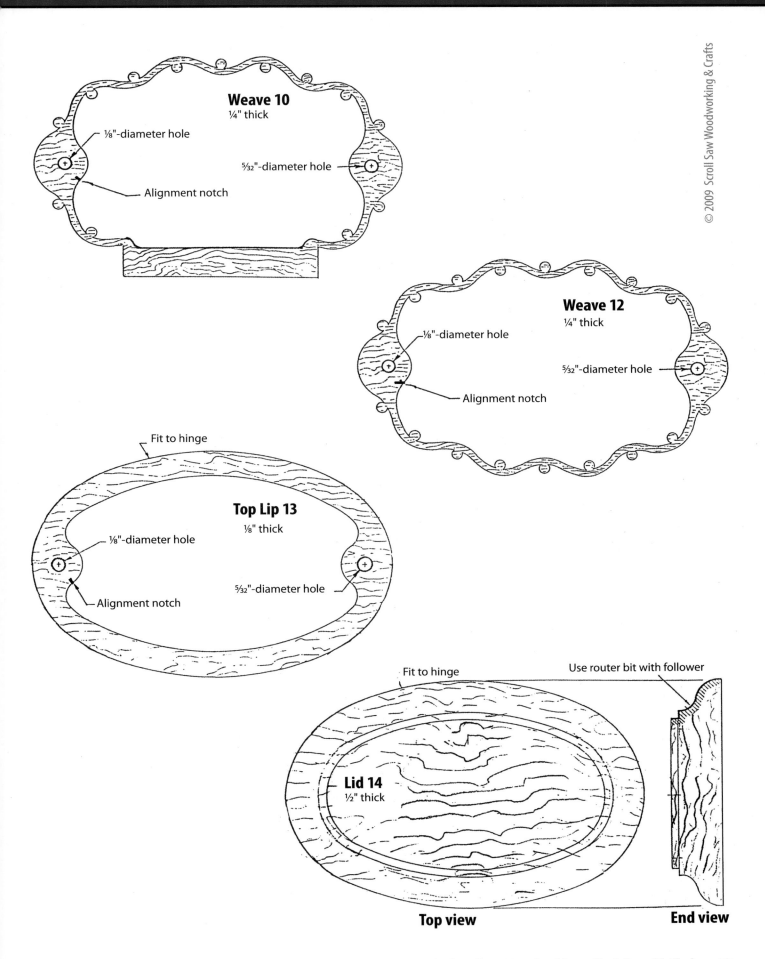

Weave 10
¼" thick

⅛"-diameter hole

⁵⁄₃₂"-diameter hole

Alignment notch

Weave 12
¼" thick

⅛"-diameter hole

⁵⁄₃₂"-diameter hole

Alignment notch

Fit to hinge

Top Lip 13
⅛" thick

⅛"-diameter hole

⁵⁄₃₂"-diameter hole

Alignment notch

Fit to hinge

Use router bit with follower

Lid 14
½" thick

Top view

End view

Octagonal Jewelry Boxes

Turn contrasting scrap wood into easy-to-make, attractive containers

By Gary MacKay

Materials & Tools

Materials:

- ¾" x 11" x 5½" walnut for box (alternatives include cherry or poplar)
- ¼" x 5½" x 5½" walnut for box bottom (alternatives include cherry or poplar)
- ½" x 5½" x 5½" walnut for lid (alternatives include cherry or poplar)
- ¼" x 5½" x 5½" poplar for lid liner (contrasting wood color alternatives include walnut, cherry, maple or oak)
- Pencil
- Temporary bond spray adhesive
- Woodworker's glue
- Old newspaper
- Masking tape
- Clear packaging tape
- Clear finish of choice
- 8½" x 11" poster board (optional)
- 8½" x 11" felt or velvet (optional)
- Sandpaper, 80 and 220 grits

Tools:

- Thick wood blade, 7 teeth per inch (TPI) or equivalent #12 blade
- #5 reverse-tooth blade
- Drill with ⅟₁₆"-diameter twist bit and ⅛"-diameter or larger diameter twist bit
- 2 screw-type bar clamps with 6" capacity
- 4 pieces, 1" x 6" x 1" scrap wood clamping blocks
- Scissors
- Old flat blade screwdriver

This simple but unique-looking box makes a great gift on its own merits or it can become a classy container for that piece of jewelry your beloved has hinted about receiving.

To save money on wood, you can make this box using surfaced poplar and oak in the dimensions and small quantities available in your local home improvement warehouse. You can enhance the look of the box by lining the compartments, using woodworker's glue, felt, and poster board, all easy to find at craft stores. Try experimenting with different wood species or turn your scrap wood into this attractive, easy-to-make project.

Step 1: Prepare the box piece of wood. Use your scroll saw and a #5 reverse-tooth blade to cut your ¾" walnut box piece of wood in half, yielding two pieces that measure 5½" x 5½". Before gluing these two pieces together, use 220-grit sandpaper to take off any wood fuzzies that will prevent the required wood-to-wood contact. Before gluing, place a single sheet of newspaper on your clamps to protect the clamps and work surface from any excess glue that squeezes out. Spread a thin layer of woodworker's glue on both pieces and clamp together with the four, scrap wood clamping blocks.

Only tighten the screw clamps with the force generated by your thumb and two fingers. It is critical that you do not screw the clamps so tight that all of the glue is forced from the glue joint. You do not need to wipe whatever glue is squeezed out. Leave the two pieces clamped overnight to dry.

Step 2: Adhere the pattern. Unclamp the box blank that you made in Step 1. Apply temporary bond spray adhesive to the back of the box pattern and adhere the pattern to the box blank. Apply clear packaging tape over the box pattern. Drill ⅛"-diameter or larger holes through each of the three compartments. With a thick wood 7 TPI blade or equivalent #12 blade, cut out the three sections to create the divided compartments. If you intend to line your box with felt or velvet, save one of the cutout sections and don't remove the paper on it.

Step 3: Secure the box bottom to the box. Apply a thin layer of woodworker's glue to the bottom of the box before placing your ¼" x 5½" x 5½" box bottom on the glued surface. Then, apply one piece of masking tape to each side of the box to secure the box bottom to the box. Using two screw-type bar clamps and four scrap wood clamping blocks, clamp the box for about ten minutes. Remove the clamps and clean out the squeezed-out glue from the bottom of the three compartments with an old flat blade screwdriver. Reclamp the box with your clamping blocks and leave overnight to dry. You can use 80-grit sandpaper to remove the glue from the screwdriver.

Step 4: Apply the pattern to the lid liner. Unclamp the box and remove the masking tape and pattern from the top. Spray the back of the lid liner pattern with temporary bond spray adhesive and apply the pattern to the ¼" x 5½" x 5½" lid liner. Cover the pattern with clear packaging tape. Drill one 1⁄16"-diameter hole between the rings on the pattern. Using a #5 blade inserted through the 1⁄16"-diameter hole, cut out the outer ring, then insert the blade back into the hole and cut out the inner ring. Using 220-grit sandpaper, sand the top of the box dividers and remove any wood fuzzies from the top of the box.

Step 5: Put the lid liner on the glued surface. Spread a thin layer of woodworker's glue on the top of the box, being careful not to get any glue on the three dividers. Place the ¼" x 5½" x 5½" lid liner on the glued surface. Clamp the box with the clamping blocks for ten minutes. Remove the clamps, clean any glue that squeezed out and reclamp the box overnight.

Step 6: Cut out the outside of the box. Unclamp the box. Using a 7 TPI blade or equivalent #12 blade, cut out the outside box, and remove the paper pattern from the top of the box.

HELP THE GLUE SET UP **TIP**

Hold the glued round lid liner in position for about one minute before clamping. This gives the glue time to set up and prevents the lid liner from sliding out of position when you clamp it.

Design Your Own Box

The accompanying illustration shows how this project pattern was designed and also indicates how to draw three other designs. You will only need a protractor, compass with lead point, sharp pencil, and paper to make your own designs.

Quadrant A shows an eight-sided box design based on each side equaling 45°. Set the compass width equal to the distance where the angle meets the outer circle and draw an arc outside the outer circle. Draw another arc from the other point. Move the compass to the point where the two arcs cross, then draw the arc that is the outside profile of your box.

Quadrant B shows a 16-sided box design based on each side equaling 22½°. Quadrant C shows a 12-sided box design based on each side equaling 30°. Quadrant D shows an eight-sided box design based on 15- and 30-degree divisions, with the outside box profile arcs drawn from the inner circle point.

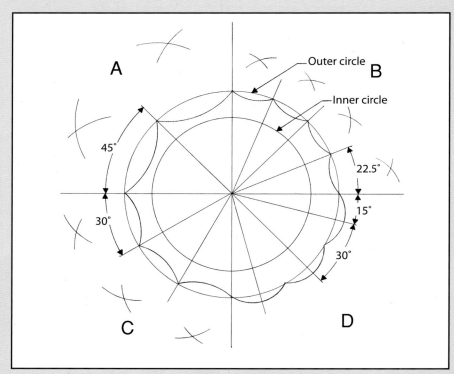

Step 7: Cut out the outside lid profile. Spray the back of the lid pattern using temporary bond spray adhesive, and apply the pattern to the ½" x 5½" x 5½" lid. Cover the surface with clear packaging tape. Cut out the outside lid profile with a #5 blade. Using 220-grit sandpaper, sand the fuzzies from the lid and round lid liner.

Photocopy at 100%

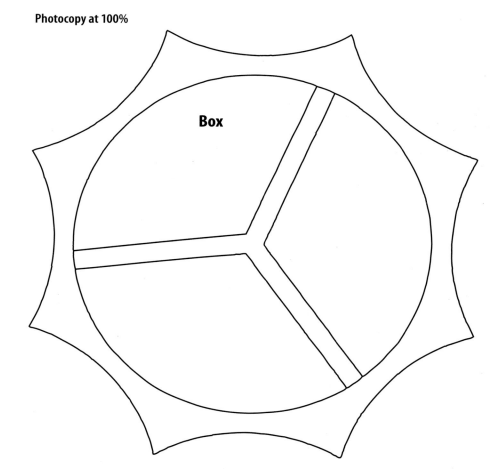

Box

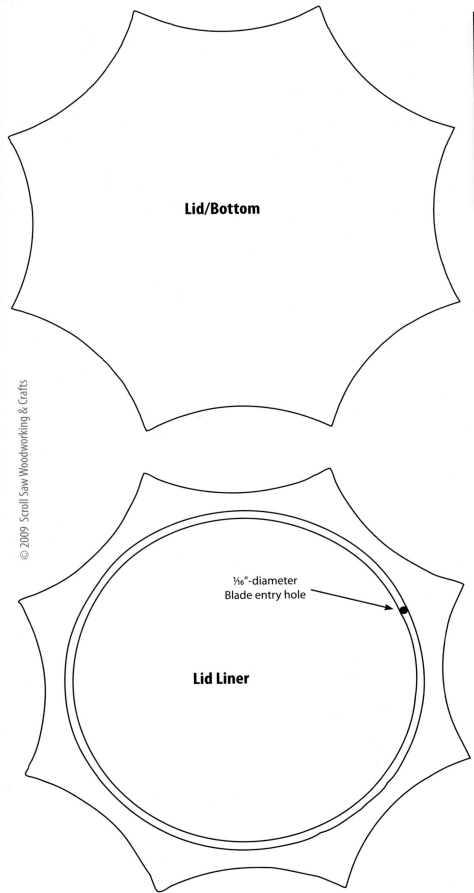

Lid/Bottom

Lid Liner

¹⁄₁₆"-diameter
Blade entry hole

Step 8: Center the lid liner on the lid. Apply a very thin layer of woodworker's glue to one side of the round lid liner and center the lid liner on the lid. Clamp the lid liner to the lid with clamping blocks, and use a screwdriver to remove glue squeezed out. Allow the clamped piece to dry overnight.

Step 9: Sand the box and lid. Unclamp the lid, remove the paper pattern, and sand the box and lid using 220-grit sandpaper. Apply a clear finish of choice. In this case, I applied one coat of shellac.

Step 10: Line the compartments (optional). To line the compartments of your jewelry box with felt or velvet, proceed this way: Place a single half sheet of newspaper on a flat surface. Place an 8½" x 11" sheet of poster board on the newspaper. Cover one side of the poster board with a layer of woodworker's glue. Roll up an 8½" x 11" piece of felt or velvet, then starting at one edge of the poster board, unroll the fabric over your glued poster board. Place a single sheet of newspaper over the fabric, then weigh it down with a few telephone directories or other catalogs. Let this work dry overnight. Using one of the scraps of wood you saved when you cut out the compartments, place the scrap paper side down on the back of the poster board and trace its outline with a sharp pencil. Trace the outline for all three compartments. Then use sharp scissors to cut out the outline. Insert your linings into the bottom of the compartments.

Monogram Keepsake Box

Simple techniques create a unique personalized gift

By Rhys Hanna

A person's name is the sweetest sound in the world to that individual. That's what makes this Monogram Keepsake Box a perfect way to show your appreciation. I make most of my boxes on the bandsaw, but I designed this project specifically for the scroll saw. This box was crafted for my daughter Kirsten as a graduation gift. She is now officially Dr. Hanna and was delighted with her gift—especially when she opened each drawer to find gold chain bracelets in them.

I start by drawing and cutting a pattern out of ⅛"-thick MDF. That way, I can decide how I want the drawers to be shaped—and make sure that when they're cut, they can be used.

Prepare your stock

While it is a trial for most scroll saws, I make my main box 2" thick. A ⁵⁄₁₆" backer board covers my cuts and makes up the rear of the box. To avoid cutting 2" thick wood, you can always cut 1" thick sections and glue them together.

Trace the pattern onto the wood, and mark the drawer cuts with an arrow pointing up. This ensures the interior of the drawer is cut correctly.

Cutting the main box

1 **Cut the outside profile of the main box body.** I use a #12 skip-tooth blade. After cutting the outside profile, orient the grain of the backing board with the box body, and trace the profile of the box body onto the backing board. Cut the backer board, using the same blade.

3 **Use the same technique to cut out the rest of the drawers.** Since the kerf (saw blade width) of the blade is so small and since scroll saw blades cut so cleanly, it is easy to glue these cuts closed later. It is also possible to drill small blade entry holes to cut out the drawers, but small-diameter drill bits—and small scroll saw blades—are going to break easily in wood this thick.

Assembly

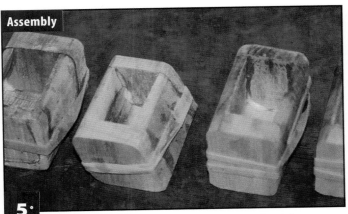

5 **Glue the front and back onto the drawers.** Sand the cut ends to ensure a tight fit. Apply a thin layer of glue to the center of the drawer, and position the front and back in place. Use rubber bands to hold the front and back in place until the glue dries.

Cutting the drawers

2 **Cut out the drawers.** Start at the bottom, and cut the whole way up to and around the top drawer. Then, turn the saw off, slide the blade back to the next lower drawer, turn the saw on, and cut around the perimeter of the drawer.

4 **Cut the drawer sections.** Cut 7/16" from the front and 1/4" from the back of each drawer. These pieces will be the front and back of the drawers. Use the arrows you drew on the pattern to ensure that you have the drawer right side up. Mark and cut the center section out of the drawer. Make sure the walls of the drawer are at least 3/16" thick.

6 **Glue up the box body.** Apply glue to the cuts in the bottom and work the glue into the joint with a knife. Apply glue around the edge of the main body and put the back in place. Clamp the pieces together. Don't glue the saw cuts through the drawer divisions—these are detailed with a V-shaped cut later.

7 **Sand the box.** I use a belt sander on the flat surfaces and a vertical oscillating sander for the rounded sections. To remove the marks from the belt sander, I use a 9"-diameter disc sander with a soft rubber backing (a computer mouse pad, see Protecting Your Finish) fitted with 220-grit sandpaper. Finally, hand sand the piece with 400-grit sandpaper.

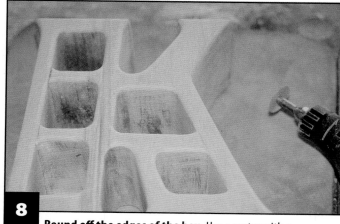

8 **Round off the edges of the box.** Use a router with a ⅛"-diameter round-over bit. The edges can be rounded with sandpaper if you prefer. Don't round off the box bottom. Round the edges of the drawers with sandpaper. Use a rotary power carver and a cut-off bit to add V-shaped cuts to accent the lines between the drawers.

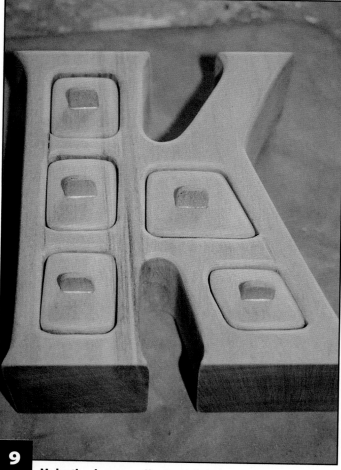

9 **Make the drawer pulls.** Cut ³⁄₁₆"-thick strips from the scrap portion of the box backer. Cut ⅝"-long pieces from the strips and round the corners on one end. I use a flap sander, but it can also be done by hand. Flatten the square end on a sander until the piece is ½" long (to make sure you have a square edge). Glue these pulls to the drawer fronts.

10 **Apply your finish of choice.** I applied a gloss lacquer, but the boxes look good with almost any finish.

11 **Line the inside of the drawers (optional).** I tint PVA glue with poster paint that matches the flocking I plan to use inside the drawers. Paint the inside of the drawer with the glue, allow it to sit a few minutes, and apply another coat of glue. Pour some of the flocking into the drawer, shake it around to make sure you cover the glue surface, and dump out the excess. After the glue dries, I use compressed air to make sure I've gotten all the extra flocking material out.

Materials:

- ⅛" x 6" x 6" MDF or plywood of choice (test pattern, optional)
- 2" x 6" x 6" hardwood of choice (main box)
- ⁵⁄₁₆" x 6" x 6" hardwood of choice (backer board)
- Assorted grits of sandpaper up to 400 grit
- Wood glue of choice
- PVA glue of choice
- Flocking color of choice
- Poster paint that matches flocking color
- Finish of choice

Tools:

- #12 skip-tooth scroll saw blades or blades of choice
- Belt sander, oscillating sander, disc sander (optional)
- Router with ⅛"-diameter round-over bit (optional)
- Assorted clamps
- Rotary power carver with cut-off bit (to highlight the V-shaped cuts)
- Small paintbrush
- Compressed air (to clean out drawers)

PROTECTING YOUR FINISH **TIP**

Old computer mouse pads offer a soft surface to protect your finished work. They are also good as a backing for sandpaper, giving you a firm yet flexible sanding surface.

LOW-COST SPINDLE SANDER **TIP**

Chuck a length of ⅜"-diameter dowel into a drill. Wrap your grit of choice around the dowel and secure it with masking tape.

A SOFTER SANDING SURFACE **TIP**

I use paint rollers with a ¼"-diameter bore around the mandrel of my vertical oscillating sander. I tape different grits of sandpaper around the roller and secure it with masking tape. This gives a slightly soft surface to sand with.

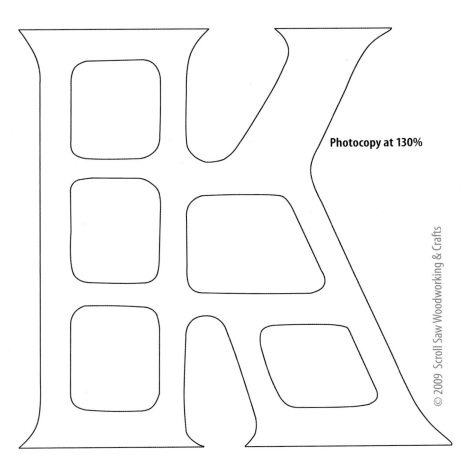

Photocopy at 130%

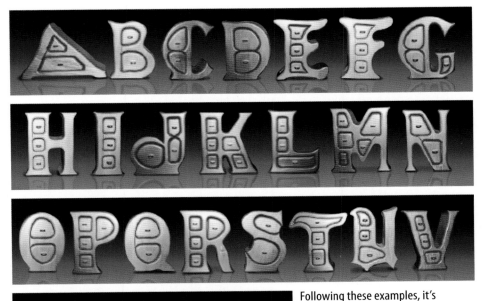

Following these examples, it's easy to design a box for every letter of the alphabet.

Woven Basket with Compound Cut Handle

A new weave technique

By John A. Nelson and Diana Thompson

Diana Thompson and I had so much fun with collaborating on previous projects that we thought we would do another project together. Diana is a lot fun to work with; if I come up with an unusual design request, she always thinks about it and comes through for me.

Anyone who has ever tried to design a compound cut project will really appreciate Diana's work. She has come up with patterns that fill four books full of compound cutting projects.

We decided to combine our efforts toward making this small basket with lid and handle. I had designed the basket but later thought it needed a special handle for the lid. A compound cut handle would be just perfect, so I contacted Diana. I thought that coming up with the handle would keep Diana busy (and hopefully out of trouble) for a while. How wrong I was—she came right back with four or five patterns for me to choose from. We both hope you like our efforts.

Step 1: Select your woods. Cut your stock according to the Materials & Tools list.

Step 2: With fine-grit sandpaper, sand lightly the top and bottom surfaces. Wipe them clean with a tack or other clean cloth.

Step 3: Adhere the patterns. Make copies of the patterns and attach them to the wood with temporary bond spray adhesive. Spray the pattern, not the wood. Adhesive applied to wood makes a very big mess.

Step 4: Drill the line-up holes. With a ⅛" bit, carefully drill the ⅛"-diameter line-up holes in each part. Do *not* drill holes in the lid.

Step 5: Drill blade entry holes. Using the same drill and bit, drill the blade entry holes where needed.

Step 6: Cut the top, base, lid, and lid liner. Use a #5 reverse-tooth blade.

Step 7: Cut the interiors of the five segments. Using the #5 blade, make a "line-up" saw kerf at the left side as shown. This will be used to line up all of the segments when you assemble the basket.

Step 8: Cut the outer oval of the segment. Cut along the dashed line marked "A."

Step 9: At the areas marked "B," cut straight in and back out. You have to make a total of 20 saw kerfs in each segment, using the #5 skip-tooth blade.

Step 10: Cut the scalloped edges. Change to a #2 skip-tooth blade to make the cuts necessary to create the scalloped edges of each segment. Though there are many ways to make these tricky cuts, we suggest using the following technique.

Position the work piece behind the blade. Carefully slide the work piece into the back of the blade so the back of the blade rests in saw kerf "B." Following the pattern line, cut to the next kerf. You can cut either to the left or to the right, depending on your personal preference. You'll create one curved edge, then cut in a relatively straight line before creating the second curved edge as you cut toward the adjacent kerf. Once the blade hits the corner, the waste wood should pop off, leaving a nice scalloped edge. Repeat the procedure 20 times for each segment.

Step 11: Cut and sand the dowels. Take a ⅛"-diameter dowel and cut it to make two pieces, each one 2¼" long. With fine-grit sandpaper, sand the dowels so they're slightly less than ⅛" in diameter. You want the segment pieces' ⅛"-diameter line-up holes to easily slide over the dowels.

Step 12: Glue the line-up dowels. On a flat surface, glue the two line-up dowels to the base. Slide one segment over the dowels and glue into place.

Step 13: Finish gluing the segments. Take the next segment, turn it over and slide it onto the two dowels. Glue into place, using just a dab of glue. Be sure the line-up saw kerfs created in Step 7 are on the same end. Continue adding the remaining segments, alternating up-down-up-down-up to get a woven effect.

Step 14: Glue the top in place. Sand the top and bottom surfaces so the dowels' ends are flush. Use clamps or rubber bands to hold the assembly tightly together until the glue sets.

Step 15: Center and glue the lid liner to the lid. Refer to the dashed lines on the base and lid pattern for placement.

Step 16: Make the compound cut handle. First, fold the pattern of the handle along the dashed line and glue the pattern to the wood with temporary bond spray adhesive.

Step 17: Drill two blade entry holes. Use a ⅛" bit. Then, make the two interior cuts of the loop using a #5 skip-tooth blade.

Step 18: Make the outside cuts along the top of the handle. Do this on the thicker of the two sides. These will be the most difficult cuts. See Make the Most Difficult Cut First for more information on why this is generally a good cutting strategy.

Step 19: Reassemble all of the pieces. Hold them together with cellophane tape.

Step 20: Finish the handle. Turn the handle 90° and make the final cut (thinnest cut last). Remove the handle—it's in there!

Step 21: Center the handle on the lid and glue in place.

Step 22: Rub the entire basket using #0000 steel wool and a motion similar to one you'd use to sand. Wipe with a cloth dampened with turpentine to clear the debris.

Step 23: Apply stain (optional). When dry, add two or three satin clear coats.

Step 24: If you would like a nice-looking interior, line it with flocking, a special material that, once applied, looks a bit like felt. See A Flocking Primer for additional information.

MAKE THE MOST DIFFICULT CUT FIRST

This simple tip is a real timesaver. No matter what project you're working on, make the most difficult cut first. If you make all of the simple cuts first and flub up the last, you just spent a lot of time very carefully preparing wood that ends up on the scrap pile.

A FLOCKING PRIMER

With all glues and finishing products, make sure you carefully read and follow the manufacturer's directions printed on every container. Here are a few pointers I've learned for using flocking:

1) Apply the flocking when the paint (or other finish) is still wet.

2) Let it dry 24–48 hours before shaking off the loose material.

3) The flocking that comes off can be reused, so gently shake the piece over a newspaper or something else that will allow you to return the flocking to its container.

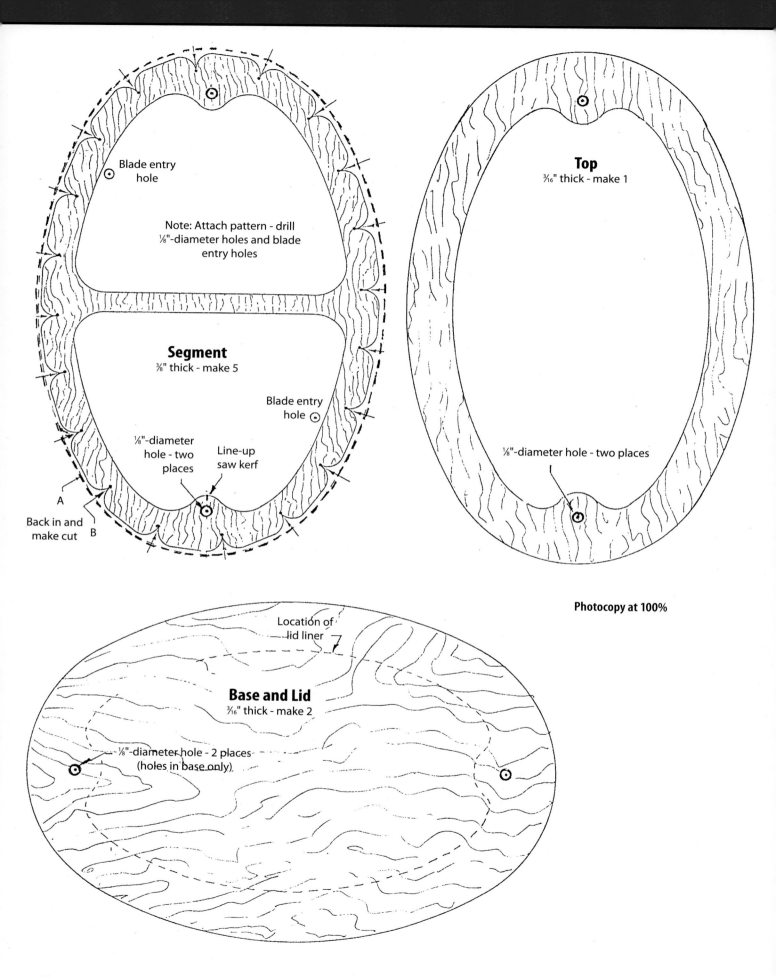

Blade entry
hole

Note: Attach pattern - drill
⅛"-diameter holes and blade
entry holes

Segment
⅜" thick - make 5

Blade entry
hole

⅛"-diameter
hole - two
places

Line-up
saw kerf

A

Back in and
make cut   B

Top
³⁄₁₆" thick - make 1

⅛"-diameter hole - two places

Photocopy at 100%

Location of
lid liner

Base and Lid
³⁄₁₆" thick - make 2

⅛"-diameter hole - 2 places
(holes in base only)

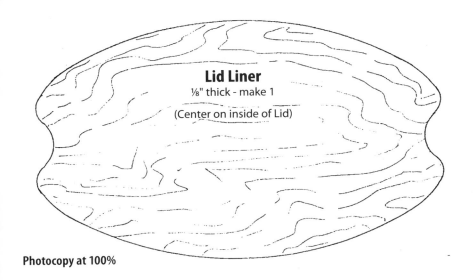

Lid Liner
⅛" thick - make 1

(Center on inside of Lid)

Photocopy at 100%

Materials &Tools

Materials:
- ³⁄₁₆" x 3¾" x 5¾" aspen (top)
- 2 pieces, ³⁄₁₆" x 3¾" x 5¾" aspen (base and lid)
- ⅛" x 2¾" x 4⅜" aspen (lid liner)
- 3 pieces, ⅜" x 4¾" x 5¾" black walnut (3 segments)
- 2 pieces, ⅜" x 4¾" x 5¾" aspen (2 segments)
- 2 pieces, ⅛" dowel, 2¼" long
- ⅞" x 1½" x 3¾" black walnut (handle)
- Flocking material
- Temporary bond spray adhesive
- Sandpaper, fine grit
- Tack cloth
- Woodworker's glue
- Cellophane tape
- Turpentine

Tools:
- #2 and #5 skip-tooth blades, #5 reverse-tooth blade
- Drill with ⅛"-diameter bits
- Clamps or rubber bands
- Steel wool, #0000

© 2009 Scroll Saw Woodworking & Crafts

Assembly

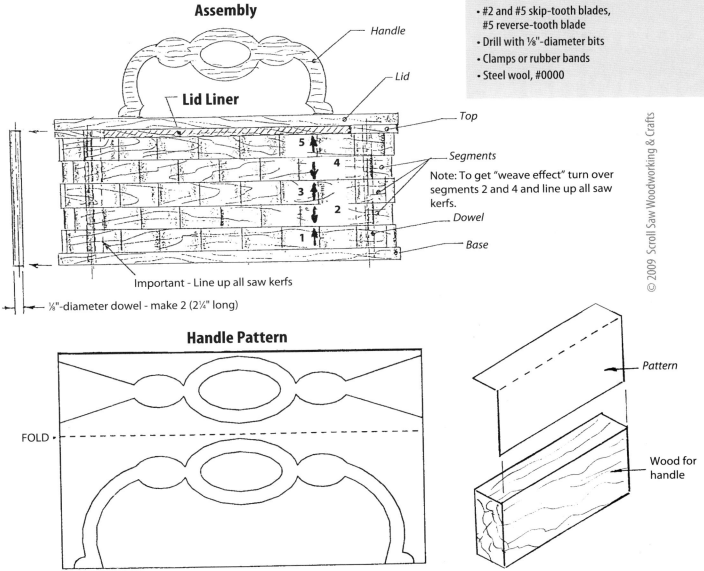

Handle

Lid Liner

Lid

Top

Segments

Note: To get "weave effect" turn over segments 2 and 4 and line up all saw kerfs.

Dowel

Base

Important - Line up all saw kerfs

⅛"-diameter dowel - make 2 (2¼" long)

Handle Pattern

FOLD

Pattern

Wood for handle

Secret Compartment Snowflake Box

Practice the inlay technique on ornaments before making the box

By Gary MacKay

Contrasting woods highlight the simple designs of these classic symbols of winter. Use the various ornament patterns to practice and refine your inlay technique before choosing the design to feature on your box.

The secret compartment is cleverly disguised, but easily opened by pulling on two of the snowflake sides. It's an ideal way to make a special presentation of a small gift.

Two copies of the inlay snowflake pattern allow you to make an individual ornament or the top for a box. To complete the box, make two copies of the snowflake box pattern.

Tilting the Saw Table

Cutting the Inlay

1 **Make a test inlay.** Attach the stock together with double-sided tape. Attach the test inlay pattern to the stack and cover with clear tape. Tilt the right side of your saw table down 1°. Drill a blade entry hole on the pattern line with a #68 drill bit. Use a #2/0 reverse-tooth blade to cut counterclockwise around the pattern. Separate the pieces and test-fit the inlay. If the top piece fits too loosely into the bottom piece, then reset your table angle to 1½° and retest. Stop testing and lock your table in place when the top piece fits flush into the bottom piece.

2 **Transfer the snowflake inlay pattern to the wood.** Use a pencil to mark centering lines on the snowflake stock and the inlay stock. Center the inlay stock on top of the snowflake stock, and attach the two pieces with double-sided tape. Trim the pattern to fit the inlay stock and apply spray adhesive to the back of the inlay pattern. Place a pin through the center of the pattern, align the point of the pin with the center point of the inlay stock, and slide the pattern down the pin, aligning the pattern with the direction arrows.

3 **Cut the inlay.** Place clear packaging tape on top of the pattern. Drill holes on the inlay pattern lines with a #68 drill bit. Cut in a counterclockwise direction with a #2/0 reverse-tooth blade to free the inlay. Separate the two stacked pieces, and use a toothpick to place wood glue onto the edges of the inlay. Then position the inlay in the corresponding holes on the snowflake stock. Re-square the scroll saw table with the blade.

4 **Sand the snowflake.** Make a sanding stock holder by gluing a ⅛"-thick cleat to a piece of ¾"-thick stock. After the glue dries, sand both sides of the inlay piece with a belt sander. If you are making a box, move on to Step 5. If you are making an ornament, use the pin method to align the ornament pattern and adhere it to the stock. Drill the ¹⁄₁₆"-diameter hanger hole. Cut the outside perimeter of the pattern with a #5 reverse-tooth blade.

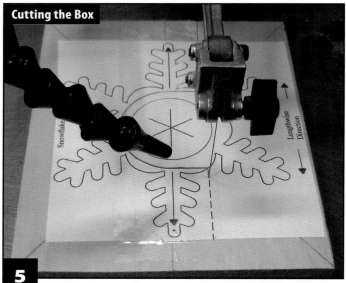

Cutting the Box

5 **Cut the drawer opening in the center box section.** Mark centering lines on the box stock. Apply spray adhesive to the back of the box pattern, and use a pin and the lengthwise direction arrows to position it on the blank. Place clear packaging tape over the pattern, and use a #5 reverse-tooth blade to cut along the dotted line on the box pattern.

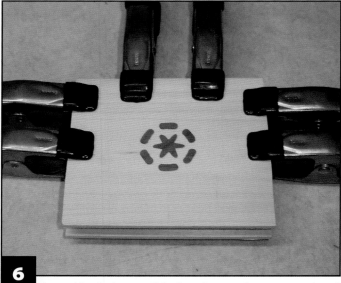

6 **Assemble the layers of the box.** Remove the pattern, and sand any burrs from the box center with the drawer compartment opening. Apply wood glue to both sides of the box center. Align the centering lines on the box center and snowflake inlay, and glue the bottom stock and inlay snowflake top to either side of the box center. Clamp the layers together with six clamps.

7 **Cut the box perimeter.** Use spray adhesive and the pin method to position the snowflake pattern on the box. Cover the pattern with clear packaging tape. Place a scrap piece of ¾"-thick wood in the open end of the box to support the thin sections. Cut the perimeter in six sections with a #5 reverse-tooth blade. Cutting in sections makes it easy to remove the scrap.

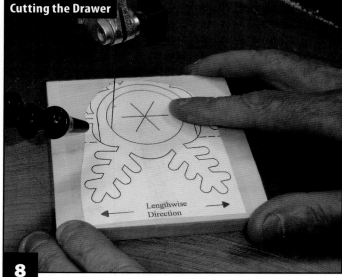

Cutting the Drawer

8 **Cut the compartment in the drawer.** Trim the box pattern to remove the four sides that are not needed. Transfer the pattern to the drawer stock. Drill a ¹⁄₁₆"-diameter blade entry hole in the drawer compartment circle, and cut out the compartment with a #5 reverse-tooth blade. DO NOT remove the pattern. Save the cut out circle if you plan to line the compartment with felt.

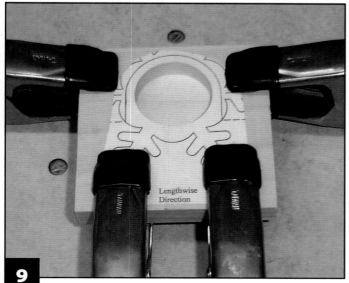

9 **Glue the bottom onto the drawer.** Apply wood glue to the back of the drawer—the side opposite the pattern. Place the drawer bottom on the glued surface, and clamp it in place with four spring clamps. Allow the glue to dry.

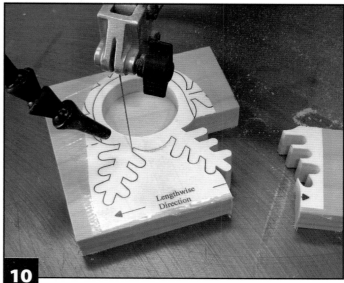

10 **Cut the drawer.** Use a #5 reverse-tooth blade to cut along the perimeter, including the dotted line on the outside of the compartment. Use a belt sander to remove some wood from the bottom of the drawer so it fits smoothly into the drawer opening.

Finishing the Box

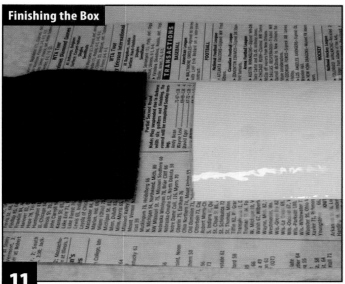

11 **Apply a finish, and line the drawer with felt.** Sand the snowflake box and drawer. Apply your clear finish of choice. To line the box drawer in felt, apply a layer of wood glue to poster board. Apply the felt to the glued surface. Place a heavy book on top of the felt, and let the glue dry overnight. Use a pencil to trace the outside edge of the cut-out left over from Step 8 on the back of the poster board. Use sharp scissors to cut out the felt and place the felt into the compartment.

Materials & Tools

Materials:
- ¼" x 5" x 6" poplar (per ornament)
- ¼" x 3" x 3" walnut (one each for inlay ornament or box top inlay)
- 2 pieces ¼" x 5" x 6" poplar (box top and bottom)
- ¾" x 5" x 6" poplar (box center)
- ¼" x 4" x 4" poplar (drawer bottom)
- ½" x 4" x 4" poplar (drawer)
- 2 pieces ¼" x 1½" x 4½" scrap wood (test inlay)
- ⅛" x 1" x 5" scrap wood (sanding jig cleat)
- ¾" x 5" x 6" scrap wood (sanding jig)
- Wood glue
- Temporary bond spray adhesive
- Double-sided tape

- Clear packaging tape
- Assorted grits of sandpaper
- 3" x 3" felt (optional, drawer lining)
- 3" x 3" poster board (optional, drawer lining)
- Clear finish of choice

Tools:
- # 2/0 and #5 reverse-tooth blades
- Drill with ¹⁄₁₆"-diameter and #68 drill bits
- Belt sander
- Pin (for pattern placement)
- Toothpick (to apply glue)
- 6 each 2" spring type or equivalent clamps
- Scissors (to trim patterns and cut felt)

Photocopy at 125%

Snowflake Box

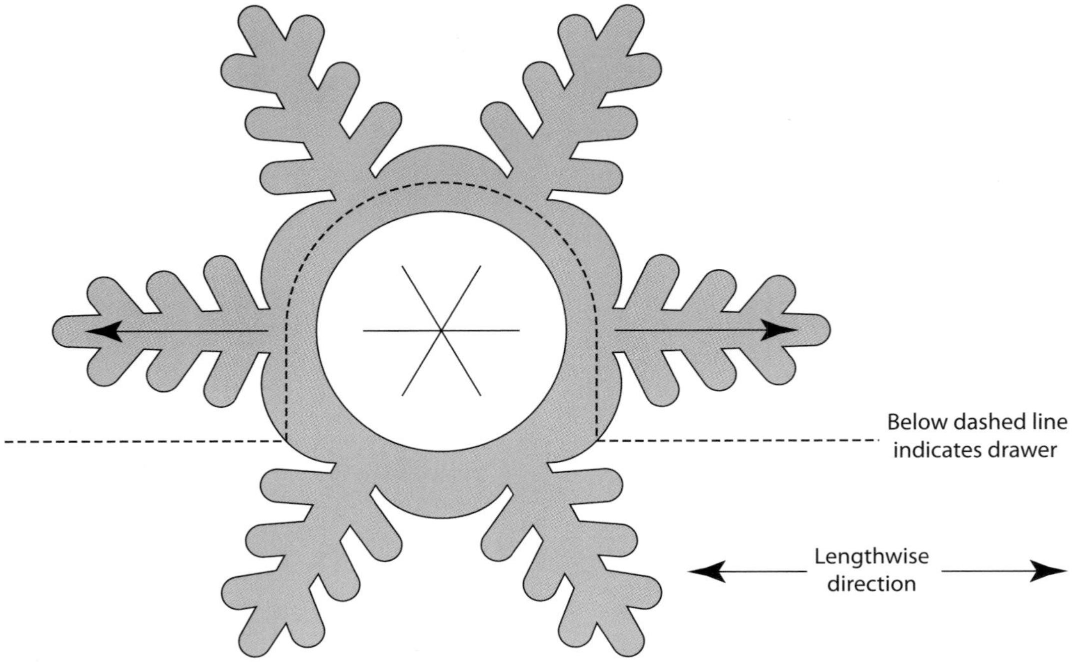
Below dashed line indicates drawer
Lengthwise direction

Snowflake 1

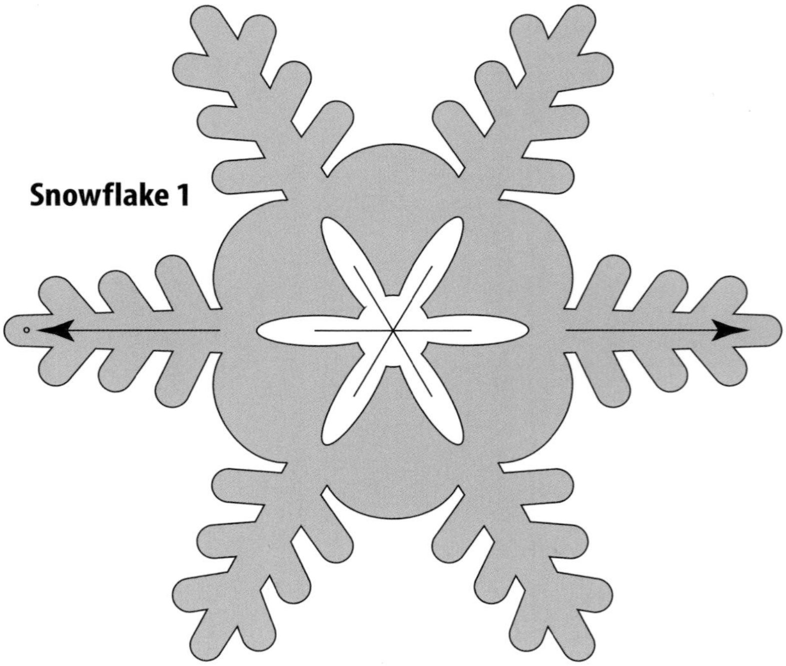

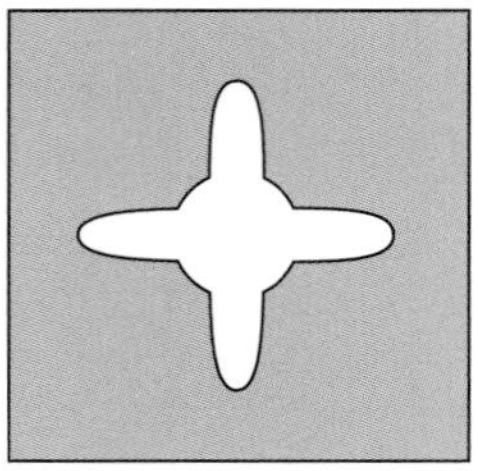

Inlay Test Pattern

Snowflake 2

Lengthwise
direction

Snowflake 3

Snowflake 4

© 2009 Scroll Saw Woodworking & Crafts

Compound Cutting

Compound cutting is a style of scrolling. Just as some woodworkers specialize in cabinet making, some scrollers specialize in compound cutting. When you cut a compound cutting project, you essentially cut one profile and then cut the second profile, and a three-dimensional image can be popped out of the blank. This section offers tips and techniques as well as projects to help you learn what compound cutting is all about.

Cutting Compound Patterns

By Diana Thompson

Compound patterns are a lot of fun to cut and produce three-dimensional projects with just a few cuts. Diana Thompson has designed countless compound patterns and has written several books on the subject. She offers the following advice for cutting compound projects.

Cutting a Compound Pattern

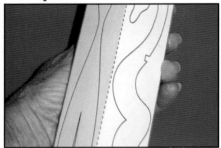

Step 1: Fold the pattern along the dotted line. Apply spray adhesive or your adhesive of choice to the back of the pattern. Align the folded line along an edge of the blank. Press the pattern onto the blank and smooth out any air pockets or bubbles. Then, wrap clear packaging tape around the blank to keep the pattern in place and to lubricate the blade. Drill any necessary blade entry holes.

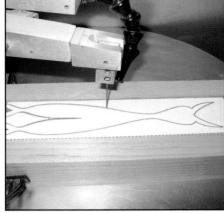

Step 2: Cut out one profile of the pattern. I clamp two pieces of scrap wood to the sides of the block. Tighten the clamps just enough to hold the piece, but not so tight that they interfere with the blade moving through the kerf. Stay on the waste side of the line. If the pattern has an open area, or fret, cut that out first. You can tape the waste area back into the block for added stability.

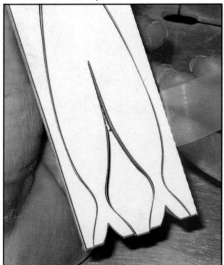

Step 3: Clamp the cutout section from the first profile back in place. Slightly pinch the figure together and tape it in place with strips of cellophane tape. Don't clamp it too tightly; just keep it from moving around.

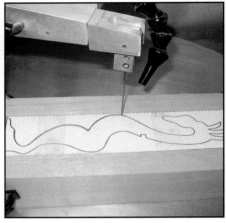

Step 4: Cut out the other profile. Use the same techniques explained in Step 2.

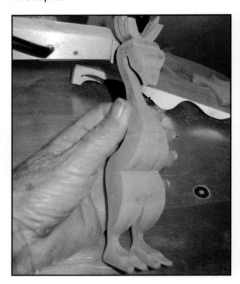

Step 5: Remove the project from the blank. Press lightly on one side to push the project out of the block. Use caution with more fragile pieces. If it gets stuck, try pushing gently from the other direction or cut off the waste area at the top of the blank; just be careful that you don't cut into the project. Once you have the project out, sand it lightly with 220-grit sandpaper to remove any fuzzies. Do not sand off the sharp corners; that is part of the charm of these projects.

A Compound Chess Set Fit for a King

Scrolling author Sam Keener takes 3-D scrolling to a new dimension, and then some

By Ayleen Stellhorn

When Sam Keener started compiling the more than 100 compound scroll saw patterns that would make up his first pattern book, a chess set was the furthest thing from his mind.

"I know a little bit about the game—just enough to make me dangerous," Keener says. "When I designed these patterns, I didn't even give a second thought to using some of the figures for a chess set." As the patterns piled up, the idea to make a complete chess set hit. The result was a unique set of compound chess set figures that make even the most seasoned scroll sawers do a double take.

If you're familiar with the game of chess, you know that there are 16 figures on a chessboard: one king, one queen, two bishops, two knights, two rooks, and eight pawns. In traditional chess sets these figures are very easily recognized—the rook is a castle, the knight is a horse, the king is the tallest figure, and so on. Sam's idea for his chess set was to break away from the stereotypical figures and create something unique.

"The figures from one chess set to another are so similar. They're all three-dimensional, and a pawn is a pawn is a pawn," Sam reasoned. "I wanted to create a one-of-a-kind set where the pieces are two-sided, three-dimensional figures."

That's where Sam's love of compound sawing came into play. About 10 years ago, when Sam was working for RBIndustries, he was part of a group of company representatives that traveled to Mexico for a show. Sam's task was to demonstrate the operation of a scroll saw by cutting out three-dimensional reindeer. A local gentleman who purchased a saw told Sam about the compound carved sculptures that were being exhibited in a nearby booth.

Each compound carving stood about 10" to 12" inches high. They were three-dimensional

This seahorse and coral piece is one of the six patterns Sam Keener developed for a compound scroll-sawn chess set. Additional patterns include Neptune/coral, mermaid/coral, angelfish/coral, dolphin/coral and diver/coral. This seahorse is a knight in the chess set.

A three-quarter view taken from slightly above this piece shows the dual nature of Sam's compound figures. Here he has paired up a cutting of the nativity with a cutting of Jesus in a crown of thorns.

in that each had height, width and depth, but they didn't feature just one subject. Each carving combined two subjects to create a type of two-in-one compound sculpture. For example, a carving of a Mexican dancer would magically morph to resemble a cactus when rotated 90°. As the viewer continued to turn the piece, he would realize that the dancer was on the front and back of the carving and the cactus was on the left and right.

Sam was intrigued and started creating his own smaller compound figures for the scroll saw. To date, he's developed hundreds of ideas that include swooping eagles paired with wary mountain lions, sailboats opposite lighthouses, Jesus backed by the nativity, and ballerinas gracefully combined with swans.

Sam admits most of the patterns are created by trial and error. He usually starts with a theme that marries two items that have something in common. He then makes sketches of each, trying to pair them up. The next step is to cut the new idea on the scroll saw. Then he repeats the process until he comes up with a workable pattern.

"Developing patterns for compound scrolling is tough," Sam admits, "Every element needs to link up." Case in point: the angel and the butterfly figure shown at right. Sam was faced with pairing up the butterfly's wings with something that would protrude from the angel. "An angel with spread wings wouldn't work, so I finally ended up with the profile of an angel ringing a bell," Keener explained.

The chess set patterns were easier than most because the coral shape that Sam was working with wasn't fixed. He altered the shape of the coral until he found a model that would fit all 16 chess pieces. The resulting patterns paired up each of the following characters with the coral: Neptune as the king, a mermaid for the queen, angelfish as the bishops, seahorses for the knights, dolphins for the rooks, and divers as the pawns.

Sam is currently working on the figures for a second chess set. Sources say that this time he'll use a swooping eagle as the background for a set of wildlife pieces. As for the king of that set . . . perhaps a 10-point buck or a roaming bison. Sam is honing the design while he's sharpening up his chess game.

Sam paired up an angel and a butterfly to create this stunning compound scroll saw piece. The front and back of the piece resemble the angel, while the two sides look like a butterfly. Only by turning the piece does the viewer realize its dual nature.

Compound Cutting Techniques and Tips from Sam Keener

"Start with the most difficult side first," Sam advises. With the chess set pieces, Sam cuts the coral first, then turns the block and cuts the opposite side. Above all, he cautions scrollers to take their time and stay as close to the pattern lines as possible. These compound patterns can be cut in any wood. Sam has used softwoods, hardwoods and even exotics. His preferred blade is a #5 or a #7.

Step 1: Cut or purchase a 1¾" x 1¾" x 4½" long block. Lightly sand all four sides and bevel or round the bottom edges.

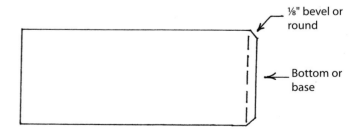

Step 2: Draw a pencil line around the block ¼" up from the base. Your pattern will rest on this line, forming the base of the piece.

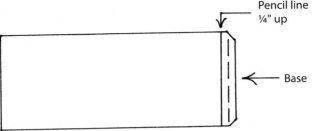

Pencil line ¼" up

Base

Step 3: Photocopy the patterns and attach them. Use a glue stick or other adhesive to attach the patterns to the block. The first pattern is glued on the side facing you. Turn the block 90° and glue the second pattern to the block.

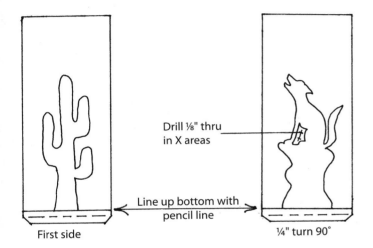

Drill ⅛" thru in X areas

Line up bottom with pencil line

First side

¼" turn 90°

Step 4: Drill blade entry holes for any inside areas that need to be cut out. Make the inside cuts.

Step 5: Make the outside cut.

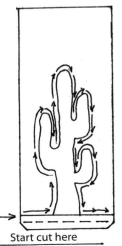

Start cut here

Step 6: Replace the pieces. Secure the block with tape.

Step 7: Cut the second side.

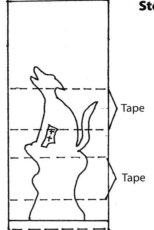

Tape

Tape

Step 8: Finish. Remove the tape and the waste pieces of wood. Lightly sand away any imperfections or tearout. Paint or finish as desired.

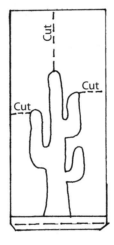

Cut

Cut

Cut

SKIP-TOOTH BLADES **TIP**

Use the largest skip-tooth blade you can for the project. Compound patterns require you to use thick wood, so a big blade is necessary. A skip-tooth blade will help to clear the sawdust.

Bishop (cut two)

Pawn (cut eight)

Rook (cut two)

Queen (cut one)

King (cut one)

Knight (cut two)

Decorative Foliage Votive Holder

Clever compound-cut design creates an elegant project

By John A. Nelson
Cut by Dale Helgerson

This simple design produces an impressive, functional project. The cutting is straightforward and assembly is a snap, making it easy to craft a large inventory in a short period of time.

I suggest an attractive, but reasonably soft wood. Maple and walnut are both good choices. Dale cut this piece from maple. If you choose a softer wood, such as poplar or basswood, you can stain the holder to match your décor. Keep in mind that you will be cutting relatively thick wood. Cutting exotic woods, such as padauk or ebony, will require more patience.

Step 1: Attach the patterns. Fold the A and B patterns along the dotted lines. Apply spray adhesive to the back of the patterns, and align the folds with the corner of the corresponding blanks. Press the pattern down, and cover it with clear packaging tape. Apply spray adhesive to the back of the C pattern, and adhere it to the corresponding blank.

Step 2: Cut the fretwork veins. Drill blade entry holes with a 1/16"-diameter drill bit. Cut the leaf veins with a #3 skip-tooth blade or your blade of choice. Complete this step for all six leaves.

Step 3: Cut part C. Drill a blade entry hole with a 1/16"-diameter drill bit. Cut the inside of part C with the same blade. Use caution to make straight cuts in the notches for easier assembly. Cut the perimeter of part C.

Step 4: Cut the leaf outlines. Set the blank on the saw table so the leaf shape faces up. Using a #5 skip-tooth blade, cut the outline of the leaf, but don't remove the leaf from the block of wood. Wrap clear packaging tape around the blank to hold the cut leaf in place.

Step 5: Cut the leaf profile. Turn the blank so the leaf profile faces up. Cut around the profile with a #5 skip-tooth blade. Use caution to make sure the cut piece doesn't shift, and cut a straight line on the section that joins the notch on part C.

Step 6: Free the cutting from inside the blank. Remove the tape, and carefully slide out the completed leaf side from each blank.

Step 7: Sand all of the pieces. Use 220-grit sandpaper to remove any rough edges or fuzzy corners.

Step 8: Dry fit the leaf sides to part C. Use the pattern for part C as a guide when positioning the leaf sides. Make sure the leaf sides fit tightly into part C. Make any necessary adjustments for a proper fit.

Step 9: Glue the project together. To avoid clamping the irregularly shaped pieces, I use cyanoacrylate (CA) glue to attach the leaf side pieces to part C.

Step 10: Finish the candle holder. Apply a coat of Danish oil and several coats of spray lacquer. Place the glass votive cup in position.

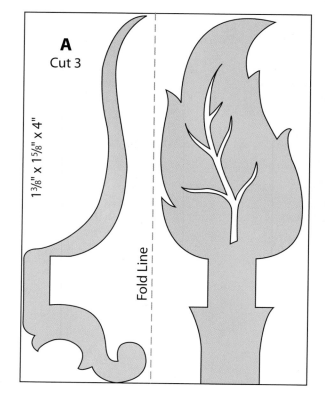

A
Cut 3

1³⁄₈" x 1⁵⁄₈" x 4"

Fold Line

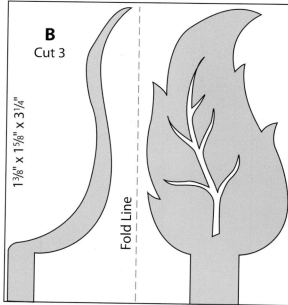

B
Cut 3

1³⁄₈" x 1⁵⁄₈" x 3¼"

Fold Line

Photocopy at 100%

Materials & Tools

Materials:
- 3 pieces 1³⁄₈" x 1⁵⁄₈" x 4" wood of choice (leaf side pieces parts A, per votive holder)
- 3 pieces 1³⁄₈" x 1⁵⁄₈" x 3¼" wood of choice (leaf side pieces parts B, per votive holder)
- ½" x 3" x 3" wood of choice (base ring part C, per votive holder)
- Spray adhesive

- Clear packaging tape
- Sandpaper, 220 grit
- Spray lacquer or finish of choice
- Votive cup (per votive holder)
- Cyanoacrylate (CA) glue or glue of choice

Tools:
- #3 and #5 skip-tooth blades
- Drill with ¹⁄₁₆"-diameter drill bit

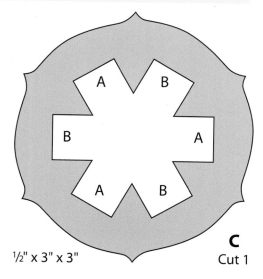

½" x 3" x 3"

C
Cut 1

Feathered Friends

Fun compound birds are easy to scroll

By John Fleig

Cut by Ben Fink

These cute little birds are quick and easy. Because they take only two to three cuts and can be made from a small piece of scrap wood, they make perfect gifts and great demonstration projects. Have a few finished birds for display and give away the demo pieces as you complete them. The excitement is sure to draw attention.

Test cutter Ben Fink cut these from Spanish cedar. I suggest a blade with 12.5 TPI.

These patterns use standard compound cutting techniques. Photocopy the pattern, fold it on the dotted line, and apply spray adhesive to the back of the pattern. Line the fold up with the corner of the block, and press it into place. Cut out one profile. Attach two pieces of scrap wood to either side of the profile you just cut to hold the cut-out piece in place. You can also tape the piece back in place. Then, cut out the other profile. Push the cut pieces out, remove the scrap pieces from the front and back, and you are left with the 3-D project.

You can paint the birds if you want, but they look great with a natural finish as well.

Materials & Tools

Materials:
- ¾" x 1½" x 4½" pine or wood of choice (for each bird)
- Finish of choice (optional)
- Spray adhesive
- Clear tape (optional)
- Thin scrap to hold the pieces in place (optional)

Tools:
- Scroll saw blades with 12.5 teeth-per-inch or blades of choice

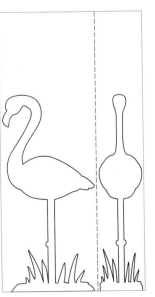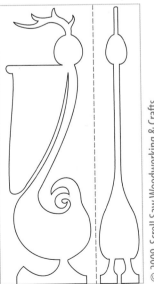

Photocopy at 150%

¼" Maple

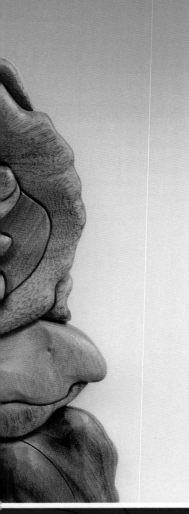

Intarsia and Segmentation

Intarsia is a popular style of woodworking in which pieces of contrasting and complementary woods are put together to form a picture. Additionally, each piece is sanded to help give the finished project depth. Segmentation projects are kind-of a cross between intarsia and relief. Like intarsia, segmentation involves a number of different pieces to create a picture. However, while some artists spend some time sanding the pieces, the process is not as involved as with intarsia. Some segmentation projects don't require any type of sanding for depth. As with relief, some segmentation projects are glued with the pieces at different heights to give the project more depth. Segmentation projects are often stained or painted, which cuts down on the need for and cost of wood with few defects and exceptional grain sometimes called for when doing intarsia.

Intarsia Puppy in a Basket

Find a home for this adorable, yet easily scrollable, puppy on your living room or den wall.

By Judy Gale Roberts and Jerry Booher

You don't have to be a dog lover to fall in love with this highly huggable and cute Jack Russell terrier puppy, nestled snugly in his western red cedar basket.

Jack Russell terriers originated in England and are characterized mostly by white with black and tan markings. Originally bred for hunting foxes, small game, and rodents, Jack Russells are loyal stablemates for horses and great around children.

The "Jack" in this pattern is indeed looking for a good home and a loving family. What's more, you'll find him a cheerful and devoted companion to your many scrolled collectibles.

Step 1: Select the wood and prepare the pattern. The Jack Russell puppy and basket need four different shades of wood to achieve a rich multidimensional effect. As shown in the photo, ¾" western red cedar was used for the different shades and aspen for the white areas. You'll need two ⅜" dowels approximately ¾" long for the eyes; we used walnut dowels in this project.

Almost any type of wood will work, but the main guidelines for this project are color and grain direction. The following are alternative woods that will work nicely: walnut for the dark sections; cherry, mahogany, or pecan for the medium shades; oak or maple for the medium-light sections; and aspen, holly, poplar, or pine for the white shades.

Make at least five copies of the pattern at 100% to make one project because you will be cutting up the pattern parts and gluing them to the wood faces. Keep one pattern as your "master," and number all the parts on this pattern. Write the same number from your master onto each of the individual paper pattern pieces.

Materials & Tools

Materials:
- Three shades of western red cedar, ¾" thick:
  - Dark: 6" by 4"
  - Medium: 7" by 4"
  - Medium-Light: 10" by 6"
- 9" by 4" piece of aspen or any white-colored wood
- Two ⅜" walnut dowels, approximately ¾" long
- ⅛" and ¼" plywood backing
- Double-sided tape
- Clear finishing material or spray acrylic
- Wiping gel
- Steel wool
- Temporary bond spray adhesive or glue stick
- Yellow wood glue
- Mirror hanger

Tools:
- 1" brush, foam or bristle
- Hobby knife with rounded blade
- #5 reverse-tooth blade
- Hot glue gun and hot-melt glue
- 80- and 120-grit sandpaper
- Mechanical pencil
- Flex drum sander, deburring tool, flexible shaft grinder, wood rasp, or 1" belt sander (optional)
- Wonder Wheel (optional)
- Woodburner (optional)

Step 2: Select a blade and begin cutting. We used a #5 reverse-skip-tooth blade for this project. The reverse teeth on the blade cut on the up stroke, which helps to decrease the tearout on the bottom of the piece.

If you use the same color board to lay out many parts, start by rough cutting them into smaller, more manageable sections.

Cut up each piece of the pattern that has a different color or grain direction. On the ML parts of the basket, the W portions of the dog's face, and the M parts of the basket's interior, the pattern parts can be cut in one section. As long as the color and grain direction are the same, you can leave these sections together. When cutting a part it's best to position the center of the blade in the center of the layout line, thus removing all of the line.

Leave about ¼" around the pattern's exterior when cutting. We generally scroll all the white sections first, then the dark, and so on. Cutting hand-sized pieces with several parts laid out on them is much easier to manage than one large board.

Start by sawing the easiest parts first. While sawing, stop often to remove the tearout. Always try to have a plan in mind when starting to cut a part so you don't end up with a very small part you are trying to hold. Make your cuts so the last piece will drop from the larger block.

The speed we use depends on the material(s) being cut. The main thing to remember is control. Intarsia requires accurate cutting, so you might want to experiment with your saw's speed to achieve the best control. We usually run about 60 to 70% of the speed range on our variable-speed saw.

Lastly, after cutting the pieces, turn them over and deburr the bottoms to remove any residual tearout. This procedure ensures the wood sits flat on the table.

Step 3: Check for fit. When all of the parts are cut and deburred, print the same number on the bottom as you have on top. Do not remove the pattern at this point. Then, assemble the parts and check to see how they fit. Leaving the paper on helps you spot fitting problems resulting from cutting outside of the pattern line.

Step 4: Making shims for sanding and raised portions. The main pattern shows the raised sections marked with an *R* and provides drawings for these pieces. Cut these pieces out of ¼" plywood and slide them under the raised parts.

While cutting out shims, we also make sanding shims, which helps sand areas in sections rather than individually. This practice makes for a more consistent contour of all the parts. On this dog, we make a sanding shim for the face, neck, and body portions.

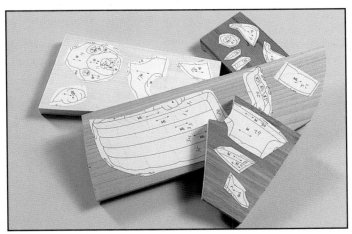

Step 1: When selecting wood for the puppy in a basket, varying shades of western red cedar work best. But feel free to experiment with different color variations of walnut, cherry, mahogany, pecan, oak, maple, aspen, holly, or pine.

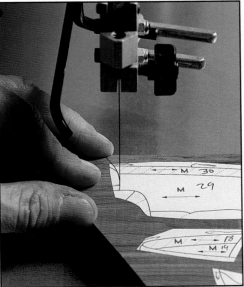

Step 2: Place the center of the blade in the center of the layout line to remove all of the pattern line.

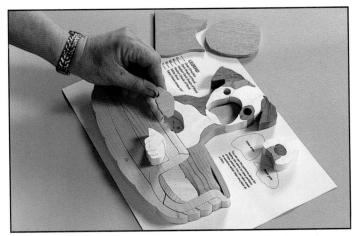

Step 4: Sanding shims for the puppy's face, neck, and body sections make for more consistent contours.

Step 5A: By lowering parts farthest from the viewer, such as the interior portion of the basket, you create a more dimensional appearance. The thickness of this section is reduced by half through sanding.

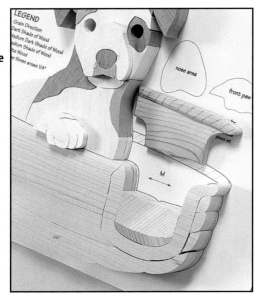

Step 5: Lower the background parts. It's best to rough in the entire project first, then come back and fine tune each part. We start with the parts that would be the farthest from the viewer. By lowering some parts and raising others, the project will start to look more dimensional. On this pattern, the back (or interior portion) of the basket would be the farthest from the viewer. Sand this part first, removing at least half the thickness of the wood.

We use a flex drum sander, one drum with 80 grit and the other equipped with 120 grit. This tool, shown in **Step 5B,** makes it easier to achieve softer contours. However, other tools and methods can be used to create the same finish. Regardless, remove most of the material with 80-grit sandpaper, and then smooth it out with 120 grit.

Step 6: Mark adjoining pieces. After you sand each part, mark the piece with a mechanical pencil where it joins other parts. These lines will be your guides. As you work your way up to the thicker areas the parts will have lines all the way around them. Try not to sand below the pencil line. If you do accidentally sand below the line in this case, for instance, sand the rear of the basket lower.

Step 7: Keep marking. Sand the back portion of the dog. Mark the chest area, and sand it just above your pencil lines. Use double-sided tape to tape the chest areas together. Put the tape on the backs of the parts, then peel off the paper, and stick the plywood to the back. This way you can sand the entire section together. Take the sanding shim off, and mark around the dog's paw. Stay above your pencil line as you sand.

Step 5B: While flex drum sanders make smoother contours, sections can be shaped with a deburring tool, flexible shaft grinder, wood rasp, or 1" belt sander. Or, the project can be left flat with softened edges.

Step 6: After each part is sanded, mark the piece with a mechanical pencil where it joins other parts.

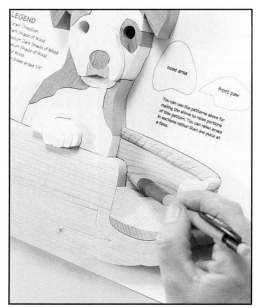

Step 7: Mark around the dog's paw, and stay above your pencil line when you sand.

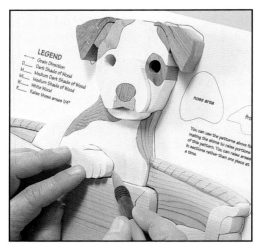

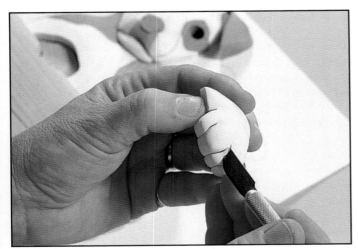

Step 8: After rounding the paw, carve between the toes with a rounded hobby knife to give them a more lifelike appearance. The nostrils can be carved in this manner too.

Step 9: Use double-sided tape and a sanding shim for the puppy's face.

Step 8: Carve the details. After the paw has been rounded, go back and carve between the toes to give them more definition. We use a rounded blade, but use whatever tools you have.

Step 9: Use double-sided tape. Use a sanding shim for the face section. Take the eyes and the nose out before applying the double-sided tape because you'll sand these parts later. When taping the face to the shim, be sure to add the raising shim to the back of the nose. Then, tape the shim along with the other face pieces to the sanding shim.

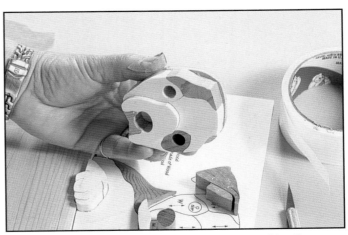

Step 10: Assemble the nose and head sections prior to blending.

Step 10: Blend the nose and head. With all the parts together, blend the upper nose area with the forehead. You can also round the upper portion of the head toward the outer edge at this time. Remove the nose section and sand the lower portion of the face. Insert the nose, and mark where the face meets the nose. Sand the outer edges of the nose, making sure to stay above your pencil line.

Step 11: Sand the ears and pillow. After blending the face section, remove it from the sanding shim. Next, mark where the face joins the ears. Sand the inner ear portion down to your pencil line; then, mark where it joins the ear's outer flap portion. Sand the outer flap portion, leaving the point on the end the thickest and taper it down toward the top of the ear. Sand the pillow portion. Watch your pencil lines to keep from sanding the pillow thinner than the back of the basket.

Step 11: After removing the blended face section from the sanding shim, use a pencil to mark where the face joins the ears.

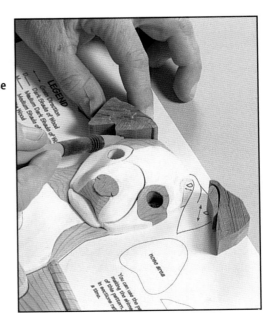

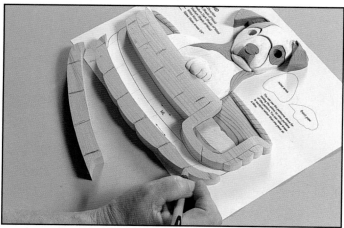

Step 12: The dashed dips in the basket section of the pattern create an alternating weave effect.

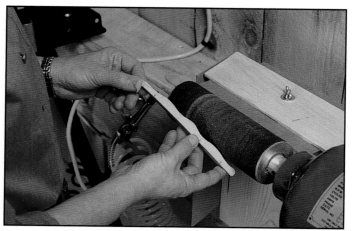

Step 13: The basket's dips can be contoured using a 2½", or smaller, drum on a flexible drum sander. However, the dips can be carved or scrolled too.

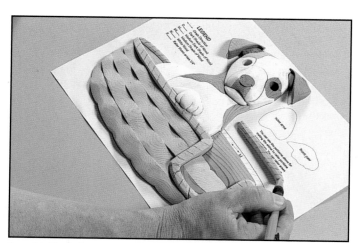

Step 14: Mark the weave lines on the basket's rim.

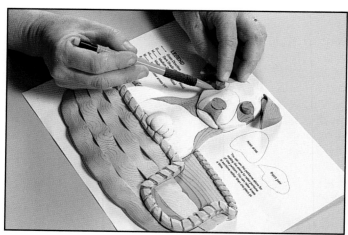

Step 15: Sand the eyes slightly below the pencil line because the eyes will be a little thinner than the area around them.

Step 12: Weave the basket. Use the pattern to mark the dips that give the basket a weave effect. Sand the basket by rounding the outer edges and tapering down toward the bottom edge. Then, mark along the bottom edge and on the face of the wood, using the dashed lines on the pattern as a guide. Marking the bottom edge will enable you to see where the dip should be after sanding the face of the wood. You will need to make sure the dips alternate.

Step 13: Sand the dips. Place the drum directly across the line to create the dip. **Step 13** shows a 2½" drum, which is about the largest diameter you can use to sand the dips. A larger width does not achieve the same affect. You also can carve these sections or perhaps turn the piece on its side and scroll the dips with your saw.

Step 14: Mark the rim's weave lines. Mark the weave lines using the same technique as above for marking the dips. We used a graphite-impregnated Wonder Wheel to make the grooves. It carves and burnishes the wood all in one stroke. These details can also be carved, gouged, or burned.

Step 15: Finish the eyes and nose. When shaping the eyes, sand them slightly below the pencil line because the eyes will be a little thinner than the area around them. What's more, we go the extra mile by adding a highlight to the eye with a small dowel-like piece of aspen, which is inserted into a small hole drilled into the eye. Cut a short section of the aspen and glue it in the hole. When the glue dries, sand it flush with the rest of the eye.

Mark around the outside edges of the nose and round the nose over to the point where the edge is sanded down to your pencil marks. The nose will be the thickest part on this project. If it's not thicker, raise it up using either a ⅛" or ¼" shim. For added detail, you can carve the nostrils by using the dashed lines on the pattern as a guide.

Step 16: Apply the finish. Described here is the finish technique we use. However, there are many finishes and techniques that can be used, so feel free to use your favorite method.

We like to apply the finish to each part before gluing the project down. For our finish, we use a wiping gel applied with a 1" disposable foam brush. Apply a heavy first coat and let it set for less than one minute. Then, wipe off the excess with a paper towel and buff it completely dry using a clean paper towel. After all parts have the first coat, allow the pieces to dry for at least six to eight hours. Apply the second coat in the same manner, and let it set for another six to eight hours.

Before the third and final coat, the "white" wood sections will need to be lightly dressed with steel wool. The gel will raise the grain slightly on white woods but not on the cedar, so your cedar parts will not have to be steel wooled. Apply and wipe the third and final coat of gel, letting these coats dry for at least four hours before going to the final step.

Step 17: Make the backing. Trace around the finished project to make the backing, rather than using the pattern. We like to trace the project on white paper using a light dusting of spray adhesive to keep the parts from moving during tracing. Then, apply the tracing to a piece of ¼" or ⅛" plywood with a spray adhesive. Cut a little to the inside of the line. We stain the edges dark, and spray the back with a clear acrylic to help seal the entire project.

I use yellow wood glue and a little hot-melt glue to affix the piece to the backing. The hot-melt glue serves as a clamp until the wood glue dries. Place the project onto the backing, making sure the pieces are aligned correctly. Then, glue a few outer pieces to lock in the entire project.

On this project, we recommend using the hot-melt glue on the lower basket ring and on the two ears. This is enough adhesive to prevent shifting as you glue the project down. Keep in mind that a little glue goes along way; there is no need to flood the glue on the back of the parts. Just a few dots across the back of each part will suffice.

Last but not least, find a centerpoint on the back and place your hanger. We use a mirror hanger.

Step 17: Before and after finishing: The final, finished mounted project is in the foreground with the unfinished piece in the background.

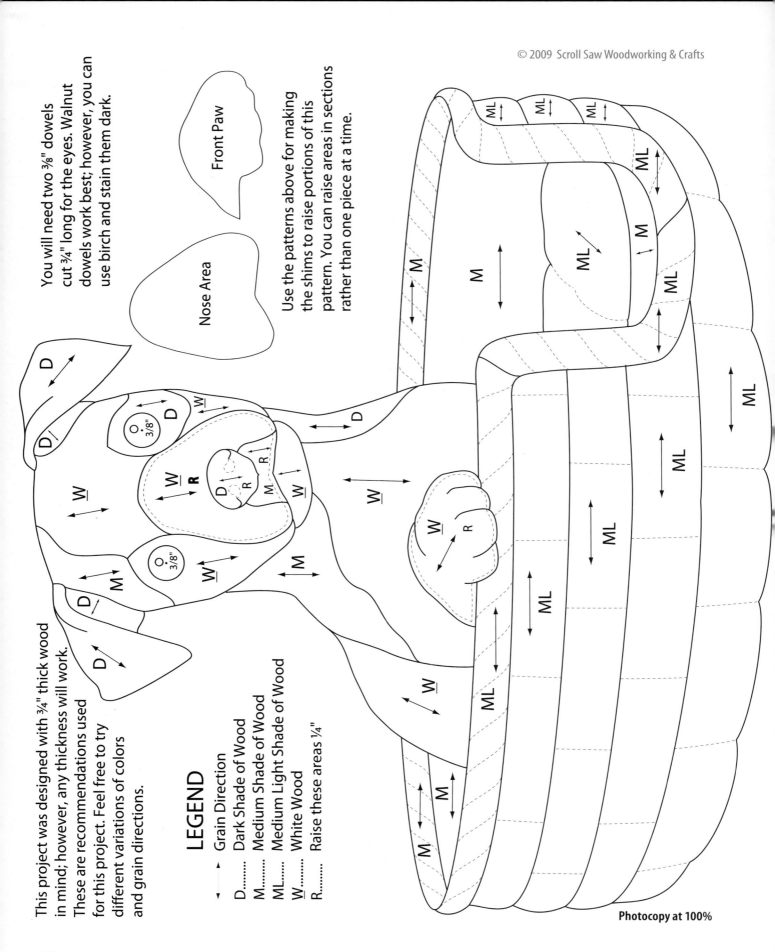

You will need two ⅜" dowels cut ¾" long for the eyes. Walnut dowels work best; however, you can use birch and stain them dark.

Front Paw

Nose Area

Use the patterns above for making the shims to raise portions of this pattern. You can raise areas in sections rather than one piece at a time.

This project was designed with ¾" thick wood in mind; however, any thickness will work. These are recommendations used for this project. Feel free to try different variations of colors and grain directions.

LEGEND
→ ...... Grain Direction
D .... Dark Shade of Wood
M .... Medium Shade of Wood
ML ...... Medium Light Shade of Wood
W .... White Wood
R .... Raise these areas ¼"

Photocopy at 100%

From Photo to Pattern: Custom Intarsia Designs

Learn to draft your own custom designs or just make this beautiful rose example

By Kathy Wise

Creating your own custom intarsia pattern is not as difficult as you may think. You don't even need a computer—all it takes is a clear photograph, some heavy, clear plastic, a permanent marker, and some patience.

I do my designing on my computer, using a drawing tablet and several expensive drawing and illustrating programs. I spend hours developing each pattern from concept to printed pattern. Many of my patterns are composites of several photos or drawings. So don't expect your first few patterns to be as intricate as mine!

I will show you a simple technique to make your own pattern from a photo using inexpensive items. If you are not interested in designing your own project, you can use the demonstration pattern to make a beautiful rose intarsia piece.

To demonstrate the process of creating a pattern from a picture, I will use a photo of a rose from my mother's rose garden and turn it into a treasured keepsake—a Mother's Day gift for my mom.

Designing a Custom Pattern

1   **Take a clear, close-up photo of your subject.** Make sure the photo was taken by you. If it was taken by someone else, get written permission to use it for your pattern. If this is the first pattern you are designing, stick with landscapes and objects. Stay away from animals and people until you have fine-tuned your skills. In addition to design skills, you need a knowledge of anatomy to make animals and people look realistic and not cartoonish.

2   **Make a larger copy of your photo.** Take your photo to a local print shop, scan it into your computer, or enlarge sections of the photo on a copier and tape them together. Adjust the photo for more contrast to help you decide where to make the color breaks. Enlarge the photo to the size you want the finished piece to be. You can incorporate elements from several different photos into one pattern. I enlarged some leaves from another photo that I will add to the design later.

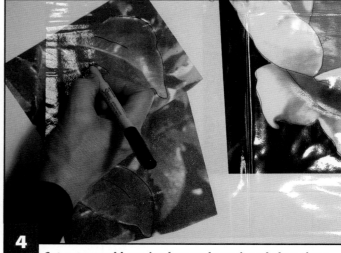

3   **Create an overlay.** Start with a sheet of clear, heavy plastic, about 4 mm-thick. I use a piece of window plastic—the same kind available at a local hardware store. Tape your enlarged photo to a smooth backer board. Lay the plastic over the photo, and use a hair dryer to smooth out any wrinkles. When the wrinkles are removed, tape the plastic over the photo. Using a permanent, black, fine line marker, trace the petals and color breaks of the rose. If you want to add another element to your photo, trace these on a piece of plastic too. If you make a mistake, use a tissue dampened with nail polish remover to erase your line. Try to make your lines flow with as little waviness as possible—that will make your pattern easier to cut.

4   **Cut out any add-ons (such as my leaves), and place them on the pattern where you think they look good.** Trace them onto your master pattern. This is where your artistic flair comes into play. If you are not sure about your placement of any added elements, ask someone else what they think about your layout. Often this second opinion will be a great help in deciding how to design your pattern. Most photos cannot be simply copied and made exactly as they are. Here you want to improve on Mother Nature and make the design your own creation.

5 **Assign the wood colors, grain direction, and depth.** Number the pattern pieces to make it easier to put the pieces back together. Start with the lightest areas of the design, and label them all "L" for light. Label all of the dark areas "D" for dark. The remaining pieces will be marked "M" for medium. I added another shade—medium dark, "MD"—for the shadows on the petals. Don't add too many shades for your first pattern. Arrows are drawn to show the grain direction of each petal. For your depth, picture the rose in your mind and determine which areas are farthest away from you. Label these areas -¼". Mark your closest areas +¼". I start with ¾"-thick wood and sand ¼" off for lower areas and add ¼" for higher areas. For higher areas, you can use thicker wood or add a shim if the area is not next to an edge. Copy your master at a print shop for a large print or on your home copier and tape the pieces together.

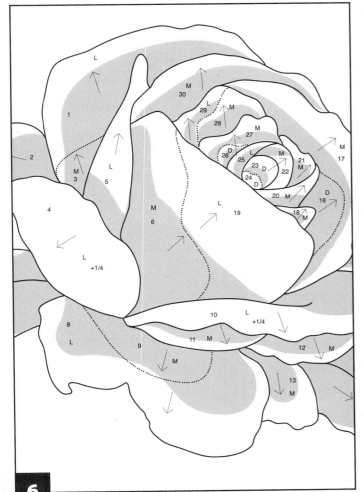

6 **Make enough copies of the pattern that you can cut out each piece individually (about 5).** Always keep a master copy for later use. Cut out and group the pattern pieces together by color. Tape the contact paper flat on a board. Spray adhesive on the pattern, and lay it out onto the contact paper. Cut out each pattern piece.

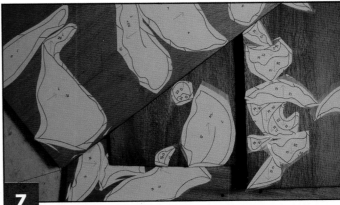

7 **Transfer the pattern to your work piece.** It is very important to pick good color and grain patterns for each intarsia piece. Your finished rose will have more character and appeal with careful planning. Peel and stick the pattern pieces onto your selected pieces of wood.

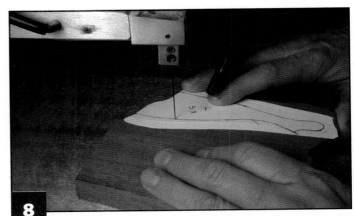

8 **Cut out the pieces.** Check to make sure your blade is square to the saw table. It is equally important that your wood is flat—so you will get a good cut and fit. Cut all of the pieces, using the thickness of wood indicated on the pattern. Number the back of each piece as you cut them.

9 **Arrange the cut pieces on a full-size pattern taped to a backing board.** Make any adjustments or changes to the way the pieces fit now.

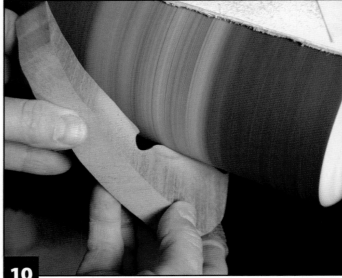

10 **Sand and shape the pieces.** I do my sanding and shaping using a pneumatic sanding drum. As you work, try to visualize the different levels of real rose petals lying next to and on top of one another. Use a sanding mop to put a sanded polish on each piece. Then cut the backing board out of ¼" plywood. Use a full-sized pattern, and cut ¹⁄₁₆" inside the pattern lines around the exterior. Sand the edges of the backing board with the sanding mop and stain just the edges.

11 **Apply a natural gel varnish to all the pieces.** Use a soft rag to hand wipe the varnish onto the piece. Be sure to cover the top and all the side edges. Let the varnish set about 5 minutes, and wipe it off. Let the finish dry overnight, and put another coat of varnish on each piece. Let the second coat dry overnight.

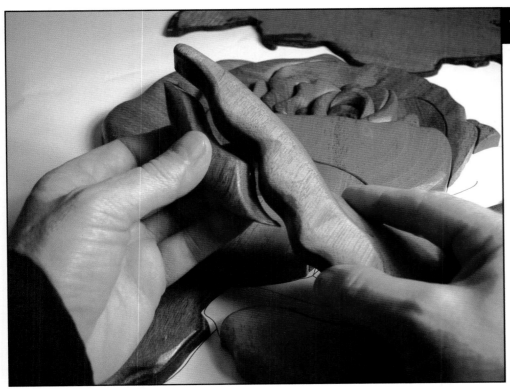

12 **Tack sections of the rose together with 100% silicone glue.** This keeps the pieces together while you glue them to the backing board. If you need to take a section apart to adjust a piece or two, the silicone glue breaks apart easily. Lay the pieces on the pattern, and tack the petals and leaves together in three sections. Be sure to follow the pattern closely. Use one or two tiny drops of silicone per piece, being careful not to let the glue push up the seam onto the front. Let the glue dry overnight.

13 **Glue the tacked-together sections to your backer board, using Titebond glue.** Clamp or weigh the sections down with sand bags. Let the glue dry overnight. Attach a saw-tooth hanger onto the back. Trim away any of the backing board that may be showing with a rotary power carver and touch up these areas with stain.

Materials & Tools

Materials:
- ¾" x 8" x 6" black walnut or your dark wood of choice (leaves)
- ¾" x 8" x 18" light mahogany or your light red wood of choice (light petals)
- ¾" x 8" x 10" medium-colored mahogany or your medium-red colored wood of choice (medium petals)
- ¼" x 15" x 13" plywood (backer board)
- Roll of clear shelf contact paper
- Spray adhesive
- Titebond glue
- Gel natural varnish & thinner
- Wiping rags
- Saw-tooth hanger
- Clear heavy plastic
- Fine-line, black, permanent marker
- Nail polish remover

Tools:
- #5 reverse-tooth blades or blades of choice
- Pneumatic drum sander
- Rotary power carver
- ½"-diameter sanding drum

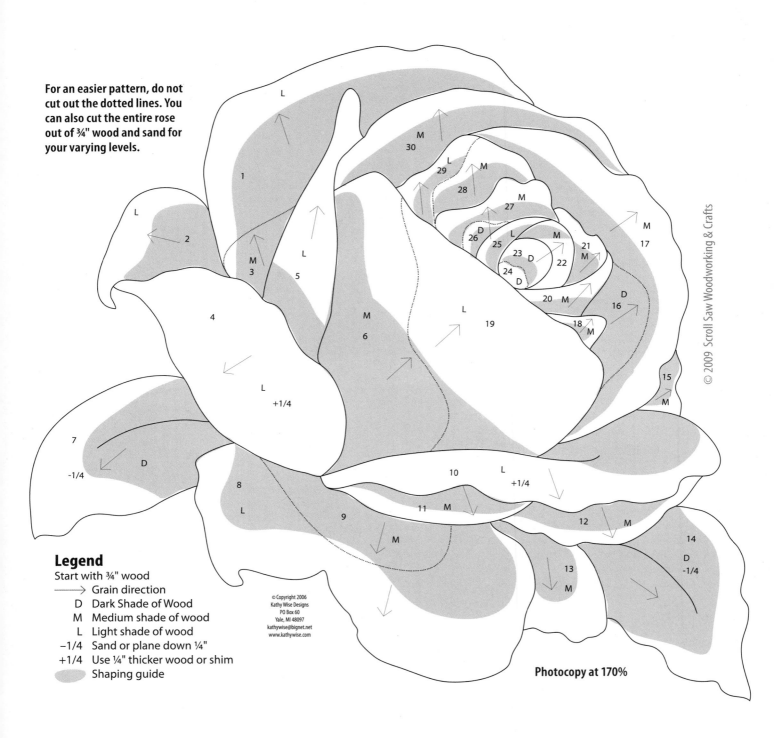

For an easier pattern, do not cut out the dotted lines. You can also cut the entire rose out of ¾" wood and sand for your varying levels.

© Copyright 2006
Kathy Wise Designs
PO Box 60
Yale, MI 48097
kathywise@bignet.net
www.kathywise.com

Photocopy at 170%

Legend
Start with ¾" wood

→   Grain direction
D   Dark Shade of Wood
M   Medium shade of wood
L   Light shade of wood
−1/4   Sand or plane down ¼"
+1/4   Use ¼" thicker wood or shim
   Shaping guide

Playful Dolphins Intarsia

Capture their charm with different woods

By Rick Gillespie

Everyone loves dolphins! Add a few pieces of exotic woods and experience the beauty and wonder of this pair and their underwater realm. The color of these natural woods attracts everyone's attention to this charming example of intarsia, making it a wonderful gift, conversation piece or great-selling item.

If you can follow a line with a scroll saw and shape the wood pieces with sandpaper, you can transform a few pieces of wood into this fascinating artwork. It's simply a matter of doing one piece at a time. I usually work with ¾"-thick hardwood or exotic wood, but you could use western red cedar or other softer woods as well.

A three-quarter view reveals the layers that comprise this aquatic charmer.

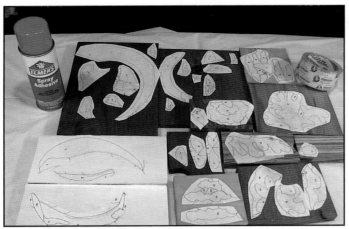

Step 1: Make copies of the pattern. Keep a master copy for later reference. After making copies, cut each section of the pattern out, leaving a ¼" to ½" margin of paper around the pattern lines. As you cut out the pattern pieces, align them on the wood with the grain running in the appropriate direction. Depending on how you want the finished piece to look, you may want to spend a little time finding the right type, color, and grain of the different woods. Once you are satisfied with the way you have laid out the pattern, attach the pattern to the wood with temporary bond spray adhesive.

Step 2: Prepare to cut. Cover the pattern with clear packaging tape to provide the blade some lubrication as it cuts. Check the blade to be sure it is 90° to the table and your blade tension is correct. I use a #5 blade for almost all ¾" wood and a #3 for anything thinner. I will use a #7 for some ¾" exotic woods, if the wood is difficult to cut or starts to burn along the edge when cut with a #5. Make sure the bottom of the wood you are cutting is smooth. Sand as needed with 220-grit sandpaper.

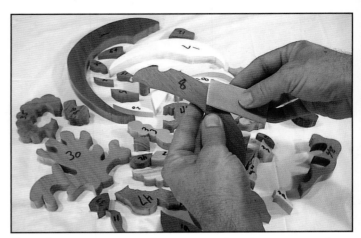

Step 3: Now you are ready to start cutting. As you cut each piece, mark the back with the same number as on the front. De-burr the back with sandpaper. Do not remove the paper pattern from the top at this point.

Step 4: Drill. After all of the pieces have been cut, drill holes for the two eyes on the dolphins using a ³⁄₁₆"-diameter drill bit for the small dolphin and a ¼"-diameter drill bit for the larger dolphin.

Step 5: Remove the pattern. Get all traces of temporary bond spray adhesive from wood pieces using mineral sprits or other adhesive removal liquid. Be safe and use disposable gloves.

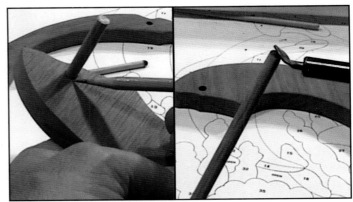

Step 6: Test fit the pieces. Once you cut all of the pieces and the pattern has been removed, put them together and see how they fit. Make any necessary adjustments by sanding the edges. An optional method is to tape two adjacent pieces together and recut the piece with a #3 blade. Once you are satisfied with the way the pieces fit together, tape them together with masking tape. Continue with each piece until all the pieces fit together.

Step 7: Decide on the thickness of each piece. Remove the masking tape and decide which pieces need to be shimmed or reduced in thickness to give a more 3-D effect. Using a belt sander, I reduced pieces 46, 47 and 48 by ¹⁄₁₆"; pieces 32, 33 and 34 by ⅛"; and pieces 21, 22, 23, 24, 25, 26, 27, 28 and 29 by ³⁄₁₆". I glued a ⅛" plywood shim to the bottom of pieces 11, 31 and 36 to increase the thickness.

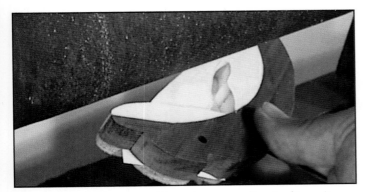

Step 8: Shape the pieces. The primary sanding tool I use is an inflatable sanding drum. Start with the main body of the small dolphin. Shape each piece until you are satisfied with the contour and shape. As you finish each part, return it to the master layout. The master layout will allow you to check the overall look and fit of the adjoining pieces.

Step 9: Hand sand. Once the rough sanding and shaping is completed, it's time to remove any remaining scratches by hand sanding. Sand each piece with sandpaper beginning with 180-grit sandpaper, and progressing to finer grits until you finish with 320-grit sandpaper.

Step 10: Make the eye. Round the end of each dowel with 220-grit sandpaper or the inflatable sanding drum. (Keeping the dowel about 6" long makes it easier to work with.) After rounding the eyes, use the flat tip of a woodburner to darken the rounded ends. An alternative method is to stain the end with wood stain or a permanent marker. Insert the dowel from the back of the head so the rounded end of the dowel is slightly above the wood surface. Mark the length and cut. Set the eyes aside until final assembly.

AN EXPLORATION OF EXOTIC WOODS **TIP**

"Exotic" hardwoods have been cherished for ages. Their names alone—rosewood, zebrawood, purpleheart, lacewood, and many others—immediately set an atmosphere of graceful elegance. "What kind of wood is that?" is usually the first question someone will ask.

The word "exotic," when applied to woods usually refers to species from subtropical and tropical regions. Most are hard, heavy, and richly colored. Many are difficult to work with. Almost all are costly, relative to the more common species. Wood that has a fancy figure may cost more. Is it worth your trouble and expense to learn how to work these woods? I believe so. I have nothing against temperate zone species, but variety and a touch of natural color can have some amazing results. Most exotics are attractive enough to be worth their cost.

There is no doubt some woods can cause an allergic reaction in some people. The question is always one of "what degree?" Each individual can react differently; some may be more prone to allergic reactions and others not so. As for me, I have not found any exotic woods I react to. Interestingly, I do have major sneezing problems whenever I cut or sand white pine. When working with any kind of woods, wear a dust mask and have adequate dust collection in your shop.

Types of Wood Used for the Playful Dolphins

Walnut: *While not considered an exotic wood, I chose walnut for the main body of the dolphins because of the color and abundance of wider boards. Walnut is noted for its rich chocolate color and beautiful grain character. As a hardwood, walnut is easy to cut and sand, but it will quickly dull your scroll saw blades.*

Holly: *The sapwood and heartwood is an ivory white color. Some heartwood may have some streaks of blue. It is especially desirable for intarsia pieces because of its irregular, tight, almost invisible grain and light color that does not degrade over time. Although it is not considered an exotic wood, it is relatively rare because the mature tree is usually small. It is found in the United States.*

Purpleheart: *This wood has a white/gray sapwood but as its name suggests, the heartwood is a bright, striking purple when freshly cut, darkening into a deeper purple with age. Its grain is usually straight but can be wavy or irregular. Purpleheart can be somewhat difficult to cut using a scroll saw. Some wood is relatively soft textured and easy to cut, and other wood is so hard it burns as you cut it. I usually use a #7 blade and plan on doing some edge sanding to remove the burn marks. Be sure to use a finish that has ultraviolet protection to prevent the color from becoming dark with exposure. It is found in Central and South America.*

Zebrawood: *A very hard wood with a somewhat coarse texture, it is distinctive for its zebra-like light and dark stripes. The heartwood is a pale golden yellow to pale brown and features dark brown to black streaks of varying widths. This wood is easy to cut and sand and finishes to a lustrous appearance. It is found in Western Africa.*

Lacewood: *This is a tan to light brown wood, with a medium- to large-flecked figure similar to quartered oak but less irregular, with a nice sheen. This wood presents an attractive pattern when used in small areas. It is fairly lightweight and cuts and sands very well. It is found in Central and South America.*

Yellowheart: *A fine, straight-grained hardwood with a bright yellow color throughout, yellowheart burns easily when cutting and is somewhat difficult to sand. This wood is great for adding accents to projects. It is found in Central America.*

Tulipwood: *This is a hard dense wood with a pinkish to yellowish heartwood possessing pronounced stripes of violet, salmon, and rose. The grain is interlocked and irregular, with a medium to fine texture and a pleasantly mild fragrance when cut. The wood is accompanied by a brilliant shine when finished. It is found in Brazil.*

Picana negra: *This wood features a spectacular background color of dark brown to red with multicolored strips varying from yellow to orange and green to dark brown. While it cuts and sands easily, it tends to dull blades quickly. It is found in Mexico and Central America.*

Peroba rosa: *While less known, this is a beautiful wood. The heartwood is rose red to yellowish, often variegated or streaked with purple or brown. Fairly easy to cut and sand, it is found in South America.*

Mesquite: *It has light red to reddish-brown heart-wood with straight to wavy darker grain. It cuts and sands easily and is found in the eastern United States.*

Step 11: Finish the individual pieces with wiping gel. Wipe the gel on each piece and wait no longer than a couple of minutes before wiping it off with a clean, lint-free rag. Wait six hours before applying a second coat and follow the manufacturer's instructions for applying additional coats of finish. In between coats, lightly go over each part with a green abrasive pad.

Step 12: Assemble the project by edge gluing the pieces. Place a piece of wax paper and the full-size pattern on top of a flat surface. The wax paper allows you to see the pattern as you glue the pieces together. Check the spacing carefully before gluing. Glue each piece together using extra thick cyanoacrylate glue. I suggest gluing the two dolphins first and then assembling the remaining pieces.

Step 13: Trace the backer. Once the project is dry and safe to handle, place the dolphins on the ¼" Baltic birch backer material. Carefully trace the outline using a pen or pencil. Be sure the outline is complete before removing the dolphins.

Step 14: Cut the backer board. Saw the plywood on the inside of the outline. Remember to take the same care in cutting the backer board as you would in cutting the main pieces. De-burr the edges and check for a final fit. Stain the backer board (front and back) black or a color of your choice. Once the backer board is dry, glue the assembled dolphins onto it using yellow wood glue.

GIVE YOUR EYES SOME HELP | TIP

I recommend using a 10X magnifier with light while cutting. Once you use one you will never make another scroll saw cut without a magnifier.

Materials & Tools

Materials:

- ¾" x 8" x 12" walnut
- ½" x 8" x 10" walnut
- ¾" x 5" x 10" holly
- ½" x 5" x 10" holly
- ¾" x 4" x 4" yellowheart
- ¾" x 5" x 5" mesquite
- ¾" x 7" x 7" peroba rosa
- ¾" x 7" x 5" lacewood
- ¾" x 5" x 3" picana negra
- ¾" x 4" x 4" purpleheart
- ¾" x 3" x 6" tulipwood
- ¾" x 2" x 2" zebrawood
- ⅛" x 12" x 18" Baltic birch plywood
- ³⁄₁₆"- and ¼"-diameter dowels x 6"
- Clear packaging tape
- Masking tape
- Double-sided tape
- Temporary bond spray adhesive or glue stick
- Disposable gloves
- Mineral sprits
- Sandpaper, 80, 120, 220 and 320 grits
- Green abrasive pad

- Clear satin finish spray with ultraviolet protection
- Clear satin wiping gel finish
- Clean lint-free wiping rags
- Cyanoacrylate glue, extra thick
- Yellow or white wood glue
- Framer's loop or sawtooth hanger
- Wax paper
- Black stain or color of choice

Tools:

- #3, #5, and # 7 reverse tooth blades
- Drill with ³⁄₁₆"- and ¼"-diameter bits
- Belt sander or suitable power sander
- Sanding sticks
- Bow sander
- Inflatable sanding drum or suitable sanding drums
- Woodburner (optional)
- 10X magnifier/light (optional)

OILY RAGS ARE DANGEROUS | TIP

Mineral spirits and similar products are hazards not to be ignored. Piles of rags soaked in volatile liquids have been known to spontaneously burst into flames. You should follow all of the manufacturer's guidelines when using any type of hazardous materials. The most common practices would include using gloves and eye protection in a well-ventilated area. Make sure you dispose of the rags in accordance with the manufacturer's instructions.

Step 15: Find the center point. You'll use it to attach a framer's loop or sawtooth hanger. An easy way to find the center point is to hold the project between your thumb and index finger until it hangs the way you want. Mark the location of your thumb on the back and attach the hanger.

Step 16: Finish. Spray several coats of a clear satin spray finish on the entire project. Ensure the spray finish you use has UV (ultraviolet) protection. Once dry, your Playful Dolphins project is ready to hang and enjoy.

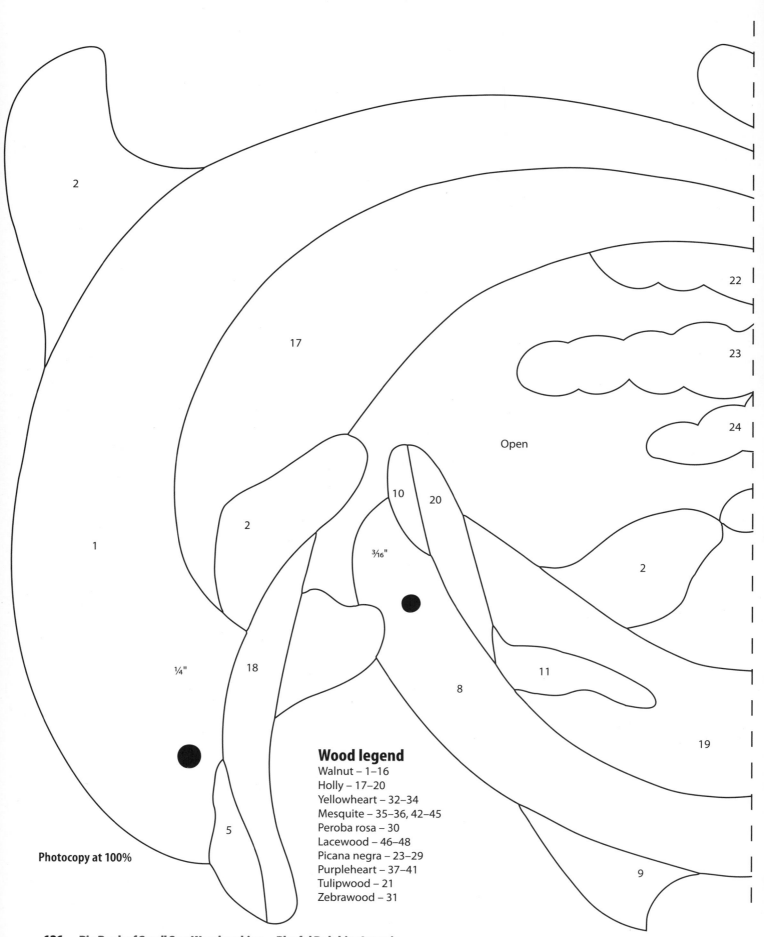

2

17

22

23

Open

24

10 20

2

$\frac{3}{16}$"

2

1

11

$\frac{1}{4}$"

18

8

19

5

Wood legend
Walnut – 1–16
Holly – 17–20
Yellowheart – 32–34
Mesquite – 35–36, 42–45
Peroba rosa – 30
Lacewood – 46–48
Picana negra – 23–29
Purpleheart – 37–41
Tulipwood – 21
Zebrawood – 31

Photocopy at 100%

9

Guardian Angel Wreath

A classic segmentation project suitable for all skill levels

By Paul Meisel
Cut by Ben Fink

Many people believe they have a guardian angel watching over them—like the angels watching over the children in this project. Many people believe everyone has their own guardian angel to look after their spiritual well-being and happiness.

The Guardian Angel Wreath is a great gift for children, and the segmentation style makes it easy for scrollers of any skill level to achieve good results. The pieces are cut from one species of wood (I use hard maple), and the edges of each piece are given a small, uniform rounding-over, or chamfer. This treatment adds separation and gives the piece dimension.

Step 1: Cut the backing board. Transfer the dashed line from the pattern to a piece of ¼"-thick Baltic birch plywood. Cut along this line.

Step 2: Cut the segmentation. Transfer the patterns to your stock. The main pattern pieces will be cut from ¼"-thick stock. Do not cut the dotted lines. The overlay pieces are cut from ⅛"-thick stock. Cut all of the pieces with a reverse-skip-tooth blade or your blade of choice and position them on a photocopy of the pattern to organize them.

Step 3: Cut the face details. Drill a ¹⁄₁₆"-diameter blade entry hole for the face details. Cut along the lines with a reverse-skip-tooth blade or your blade of choice. Switch to a spiral blade, and re-cut along the same saw kerf to widen the slot. Spiral blades are easier to control when you follow an established cut.

Step 4: Drill the eye holes. Use a ¹⁄₁₆"-diameter drill bit for the doll's eyes, and a ⁵⁄₆₄"-diameter drill bit for the bear's eyes.

Step 5: Sand the pieces. Sand the larger parts with a drum sander. Start with 80-grit sandpaper, then move to 120 grit. The drum sander gives you better control and makes it easier to sand off a uniform amount. A sanding drum in a drill press also works well. For safety, hand sand the parts that are too small to hold against the drum sander, using the same progression of grits.

Step 6: Glue the parts in position. Dry fit the pieces on the backing board to check the fit. Make any adjustments necessary, then glue them to the backing board with wood glue. Clamp the pieces in place with small spring clamps.

Step 7: Apply a finish. Start with a coat of sanding sealer. Allow the sealer to dry. Sand the piece with 220-grit sandpaper. Apply a polyurethane varnish and add a hanger to the back. You can embellish the top of the wreath with a raffia bow.

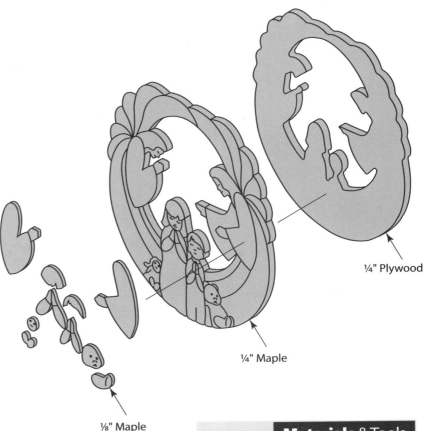

¼" Plywood

¼" Maple

⅛" Maple

Photocopy at 200%

© 2009 Scroll Saw Woodworking & Crafts

Segmentation cuts on main layer
Outline cut for backer board
Position for ⅛"overlay segments

Tiger Portrait

Segmentation gives this project a realistic look

By Neal Moore

This project uses a technique called segmentation portraiture. I believe Kerry Shirts and Pat Spielman originated it; it combines scroll sawing and wood staining to create realistic portraits in relief.

I like segmentation because, unlike traditional intarsia, I'm not limited by the colors found in natural wood. Using these techniques, I can stain the wood to achieve just about any color I need. I also like the way some of the pieces resemble loose oil paintings—when you're up close, a lot of them don't make sense but when you step back a few feet, everything falls into perspective and the 3-D relief just jumps out at you.

I love animals, so when I come across a photo that inspires me I draw the pattern as I see it. I really liked the tiger's regal pose that the photographer captured and thought it would make a great portrait. The project really isn't difficult to complete, and when suitably framed and displayed, is a work of art anyone can appreciate.

INEXPENSIVE FRAMING **TIP**

I use a type of wood trim called false tread molding to construct my frames. It is used for trimming the front of stair treads. At 1¼" thick by 1¹³⁄₁₆" wide, it has a deep face and nice profile that makes it perfect for framing portraits.

Rabbet out this section

Start by cutting the miters so the thick side of the molding faces the inside of the frame. There is a ¼"-deep channel milled into the back of the molding, but you will need to enlarge this channel into a ½"-deep and ½"-wide rabbet to make room for your backing board. I attach the backer with small nails.

False tread molding is available in oak and poplar. The poplar is not as expensive as oak and can be stained to look like nearly any species of wood.

Step 1: Make sure the table is square to the blade.

Step 2: Trim the paper pattern to size. Leave ½" of paper outside the pattern lines. Then, transfer the pattern to your blank.

Step 3: Cut the excess wood up to the pattern (½" outside the pattern lines). This removes the corners and makes the work piece more manageable. Use the #5 blade.

Step 4: Cut the tiger's left shoulder off. Cut along the line on the tiger's stripe between the neck and left shoulder. If your blade moves off the line, don't back up and start over. Just ease the blade back on course. There are few straight lines in nature and the integrity of the pattern will still be intact. If you back up and start again, you will leave a gap from the saw kerf, which could be noticeable in the finished work.

Step 5: Cut off the tiger's right shoulder using the same technique. Put both shoulders aside for now.

Step 6: Cut off the right ear using the #2 blade. Then, cut off the left ear. Leave the waste material intact—the waste gives you something to hold on to when cutting the individual segments for the ear.

Step 7: Cut the individual segments of the ears and shoulders by following the pattern lines. Cut several segments and re-assemble them as you go on one of the pieces of luan—that way it's less of a puzzle to put together later, and you won't lose any pieces.

Step 8: Cut out the rest of the segments. Work from the outside in. Try to cut the whiskers out as soon as possible to prevent them from breaking off. Plan each cut because you need to know where the blade will exit. Remember, there is no waste within the pattern itself, and each segment represents an integral part of the whole image. You don't want to wind up with a piece of the pattern so small that it's impossible to cut out.

Step 9: Pierce cut the eyes. Drill a blade entry hole right on the line between the dark eyeball and the black stripe around the eye. Cut the eyeball out with the #2 blade. Remove the other two segments of the eye in order. This way, you only need one hole for each eye.

Step 10: Drill the blade entry holes for the stripes. These should be right on the line as well. Then, cut out the stripes. When the piece is stained and assembled, the holes will be almost invisible.

Step 11: Dip all of the light areas of the tiger's face (as shown on the pattern) in golden oak stain. Do not stain the whiskers. Immediately wipe the pieces as dry as possible.

Step 12: Dip the stripes in dark walnut stain. Place them on an old towel, and allow them to air dry.

Step 13: Stain the remaining segments. Start at the bottom of the image. See the finishing guide for specific instructions.

Step 14: Lay out the portrait and glue the pieces together. Do not glue them to the backer board yet. Elevate the edges of some of the segments above the others to give the portrait some relief. Because I use hot glue, I put a dot of glue on the pieces and simply hold them together until the glue dries. If you use traditional glue, you may need to clamp the pieces together or place shims under the pieces you want to elevate until the glue dries. The pieces that would be closer to you on a real tiger are elevated so they are closer to you when viewing the project from the front. Raise the black stripes about ⅛" to accentuate the furry look created by the shadows cast by the relief. The black segments in the nose and mouth were recessed about ⅛". I also recessed the eyes slightly

Materials & Tools

Materials:
- ½" x 17" x 19" soft, light-colored wood (portrait)
- 2 pieces ¼" x 20" x 20" luan (backing board and layout board)
- Stain: dark walnut, golden oak, and colonial maple
- White paint
- Toothpicks
- Cotton swabs
- Disposable foam paintbrushes
- Disposable aluminum baking pan
- Temporary bond spray adhesive (optional)
- Old towel or rags

Tools:
- #2 and #5 blades or blades of choice
- Scissors (to trim pattern)
- Hot-melt glue gun with glue

FINISHING GUIDE **TIP**

The pieces are completely stained and set aside to dry for a couple days.

- *Orange-hued areas: Coat the segment with golden oak and immediately wipe it off. Smear and blend a light coat of colonial maple over the damp golden oak using a shading brush, cotton swab, or a finger. Smear and blend until it looks right.*

- *Nose: Dip it in colonial maple, and allow it to air dry. Smear a little golden oak along the top edge for contrast.*

- *Small segment above the tip of the nose, below the bridge of the nose: Dip it in golden oak, and allow it to dry.*

- *Bridge of the nose: I accidentally got the right color for this part. I intended to use wet golden oak on the bridge of the nose and then smear dark walnut on the upper part to get the dark shading I needed. I put too much dark walnut on it, and it ran everywhere. I tipped the piece up to try to let some of the walnut run off, and it came out just the color I wanted.*

- *Dark part under black eyeball: Dip it in golden oak, and smear on a little dark walnut.*

- *Light part of eye: Dip it in golden oak.*

- *White in eyes: Use white paint on a small brush or toothpick to add the small dots.*

by gluing them in place a little lower than the surrounding segments. When the piece is viewed from a distance, the shadows tend to soften the overall impression, and the hard edges seem to disappear.

Step 15: Add a backing board to the portrait. Use ¼"-thick luan stained to compliment the tiger. Apply several beads of clear silicon adhesive to the back of the image and press it into position on the backing board. Place a heavy object on the portrait to hold it in place until the silicon dries. Frame as desired.

Photocopy at 200%

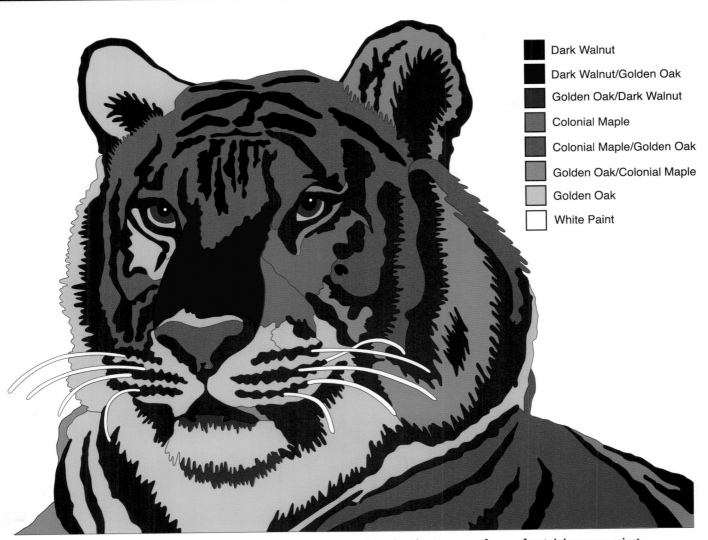

Dark Walnut

Dark Walnut/Golden Oak

Golden Oak/Dark Walnut

Colonial Maple

Colonial Maple/Golden Oak

Golden Oak/Colonial Maple

Golden Oak

White Paint

Use this colored pattern as reference for staining your project.

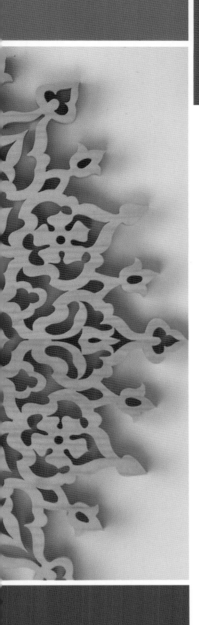

Fretwork

Fretwork is another style of scrolling. Fretwork pieces are characterized by their often large amounts of inside cuts and their sometimes delicate and difficult look. Projects can include any number of functional or decorative items. Try fretwork using the tips, techniques, and projects included in this section.

Fretwork Basics

It's all just one cut at a time

By Rick Hutcheson

Photography by Hetherington Photography

This Russell clock is a fine example of fretwork. It looks complicated, but it's all just one cut at a time. Rick designed the pattern, and Pat Lupori cut it.

Chances are, the first time you saw a fretwork piece, your first thought was, "Wow." And the second was "I could never do that." That's where you're wrong, my friend. With just a few pointers and patience, you can scroll even the most complex fretwork design. It's all just one cut at a time. And it all begins with the blade entry holes. These holes, also known as pilot holes, will be the focus of much of this article.

Select the Wood

After choosing the pattern we want to cut, the next step is to select the wood. Take a minute to examine the pattern and wood grain. Many times there are grains or defects in the wood that could complement the pattern. Try to imagine the colors and grains of the wood that would be left on the final piece after cutting is complete. It is surprising how much you can change the looks of a piece just with the grain.

You want to take advantage of the wood grain when positioning the pattern. Because grain direction won't affect the cutting action of the blade, you are concerned only with how the piece will look when it's completed.

Drill the Holes

With the pattern applied, it is time to drill the holes. The size of the areas to be cut out determines the size of the drill bit you'll need. The bit needs to be smaller than the area to cut out, but large enough to feed the blade into. Usually, the largest bit I use is a ¼" because it creates a hole that is more than large enough to feed a blade through. Other good choices to have in your kit are ⅛" and ¹⁄₁₆" drill bits. These will work well in most areas.

For the even smaller areas, there are mini drill bits, which can be purchased as a set or individually. These range in size from .0139 up to .039, compared to a ¹⁄₁₆" drill bit, which is .0652. Some drill chucks will hold the larger mini bits just

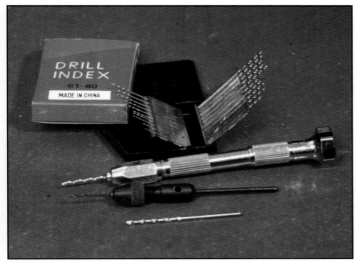

A 1/16" drill bit is shown on the bottom, for size comparison. This hand vise works well on thin woods. The complete set of pin drills are shown in its box.

The type of blade you use will have a lot of bearing on the size of the blade entry hole. The blade on the right is a # 2 blade, and it requires a 1/16" hole. The blade in the middle is a regular pin-end blade. It needs a 5/32" hole. The blade on the left has had its pin removed. With the pin out of the way, we can go down to a 7/64" hole.

fine, but normally for the really tiny sizes, you will need a pin vise, available from the same sources as the bits. A pin vise is a miniature drill bit chuck with a larger shank on it. The larger shank is chucked into your drill chuck, and then the mini bit is chucked into the pin vise chuck.

Drilling the holes in the right place can be a time saver when you start cutting. If you drill the hole in the center of

the area, you will be cutting through a lot of waste wood just to get to the cutting line on the pattern. Usually, at a corner or along the straight line are good choices for hole placement. The hole should be near the cutting line but not so close that you nick the cutting line.

Drilling can be accomplished in many ways. You might use a cordless or electric drill. A step higher would be a drill press. I prefer moto tools. These little tools will hold small drill bits with the use of the right size of collets. They are lightweight, fast, and easy to maneuver around the work piece as you drill the holes.

After all of the holes are drilled, it is time to start cutting. If you are using a saw that requires pin-end blades, larger holes are needed to get the pin through. The pin is longer than the blade is wide, so it takes a larger hole for the pin than just the bare blade. To work around the pin limitation, you can remove the pin and replace it with a safety pin. (Use a hammer and punch to drive the pin out from the top of the blade. It's best if you place the pin against a piece of wood. Once you strike the pin, it will leave the blade and stay in the wood.) The plain-end blades can be fed through a lot smaller hole and come in smaller sizes, allowing you to cut finer detail.

Different saws, because of the blade clamp design, require different ways to thread the blade. For most saws, you will release the blade from the top clamp and feed the blade up from the bottom of the wood. The best way I find to do this is raise the arm up to the top position. Slide the wood under the arm so the hole you are trying to feed the blade into is under the top blade clamp. Now, grab the end of the blade between the wood and table and flex it around to feed the top end through the hole. Blades take a lot of flexing without breaking. With bottom-threading saws, seeing the hole can be a problem. The Olson Saw Company makes a light that

PLACING BLADE ENTRY HOLES TIP

With the hole here, you are starting close to the pattern line to be cut.

If you drill in the center, you need to cut a lot of scrap just to get to the line.

In a pattern with small areas to remove, the hole placement is not as important. But in larger patterns with a lot of waste area, a hole placed in the center means you need to do a lot of extra cutting just to get to the line. But do not get the holes so close to the line that you leave a nick in the finished work.

On most saws, like the Delta Q3, you feed the blade in from the bottom.

mounts under the table. The light shines through a hole you have drilled into the table onto the bottom of the wood, making the hole easier to see.

Seeing the hole is generally not a problem with top-threading saws. After releasing the tension, release the blade from the bottom clamp. As you raise the top arm, the blade lifts up out of the wood. Slide the next hole in the wood into alignment with the hole in the table, then feed the bottom end of the blade into the hole as you lower the arm. Then, clamp the blade back into the lower clamp. On a few saws, both the top and bottom clamp can be removed. Remove one clamp and feed the blade through the wood; then, install the clamp on the other end of the blade. Now, the wood and blade, with clamps on both ends, is fed through the slot in the table, inserting the clamps into the blade clamp holders on the arms of the saw.

Regardless of the type of saw you have and how you change the blades, the same thing is accomplished: You end up with the blade threaded through the hole so you can make the next cut. You just cut that area out, release the blade, and do it all over again. Before you realize it, the project is completed.

On the Dewalt, you can feed the blade in from the top, while the work is lying on the table.

BLADE ENTRY HOLES FOR STACK CUTS **TIP**

To maximize your yield when stack cutting, you want all of your layers to be perfect. They won't be if your entry holes are at an angle as they go through the stack. Your best bet is to use a drill press. If you don't have a drill press, then make extra sure that your drill bit goes straight into the wood. And, for best results, always drill into a backer. Any tearout will be in the backer and not in the bottom layer of your stack.

ATTACHING THE PATTERN **TIP**

The easiest way is to photocopy it and attach with spray glue. All of the sprays seem to work differently, so practice is the secret to success. If you cannot get the pattern off the wood after cutting, try heating it with a heat gun, or spraying it with paint thinner or lacquer thinner. If the patterns fall off the wood before you are done, you probably let the glue dry too long before applying the pattern.

Classic Corner Shelf

Stack cutting makes this functional project easy to complete

By Bob Duncan
Designed by John Nelson
Cut by Ernest Lang

This traditional Victorian design provides a great way to display collectibles or scrolled items. Choose a wood to accent your room or one that will show off your display to the best advantage. Because the sides are stack cut, it doesn't matter if you stray from the lines a little bit—both pieces will look exactly the same!

Step 1: Prepare your stock. Cut the pieces to the dimensions in the materials list. Sand the pieces with progressively finer grits of sandpaper up to 220 grit.

Step 2: Organize your blanks for stack cutting. Stack the two side blanks and lower shelves. Because one side piece will be cut thinner than the other to allow for the butt joint, use double-sided tape or brads nailed through waste areas. Use your method of choice to stack the lower shelves.

Step 3: Transfer the pattern to your work piece using your method of choice. Drill blade entry holes for the interior cuts. Use a 1/16"-diameter drill bit for most of the interior cuts. For the veining details, use the smallest-diameter drill bit that a #2/0 blade will fit through. Drill 1/64"-diameter holes to join the sides and for the shelves where indicated on the pattern.

Step 4: Cut the veining details. Use a #2/0 reverse-tooth blade. Make the other interior cuts using a #1 reverse-tooth blade.

Step 5: Cut out the perimeter of the sides. Use a #3 reverse-tooth blade. Cut out the shelves. If you find it difficult to cut the curves, cut outside the lines and sand them to shape.

Step 6: Assemble the shelves. Apply a bead of wood glue along the end grain of the thinner side piece. Line up the piece and hold it in place while you drive the small brads into place. Allow the glue to dry overnight. Apply glue to the square ends of the shelves, line them up, and nail them in place as well.

Step 7: Apply your clear spray finish of choice.

Materials &Tools

Materials:
- 1/4" x 4 1/2" x 16" wood of choice (thin side piece)
- 1/4" x 4 3/4" x 16" wood of choice (wide side piece)
- 1/4" x 4" x 4" wood of choice (top shelf)
- 2 pieces 1/4" x 5" x 5" wood of choice (middle and bottom shelves)
- Small brads of choice
- Double-sided tape
- Assorted grits of sandpaper
- Wood glue of choice
- Adhesive of choice (to attach pattern to blank)
- Clear spray finish of choice

Tools:
- #2/0, #1, and #3 reverse-tooth blades or blades of choice
- Drill with assorted small drill bits
- Hammer

Photocopy at 170%

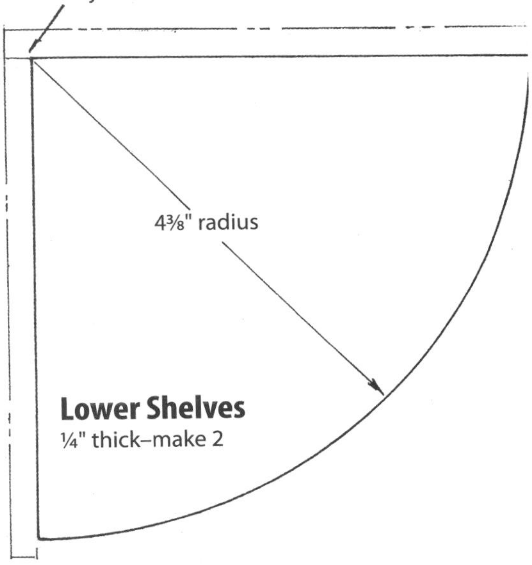

Top Shelf
3⁷⁄₈" radius

3⁷⁄₈" radius

Shelf

¹⁄₆₄" diameter hole–as shown

Butt joint

Shelf

Lower Shelves
¼" thick–make 2

4³⁄₈" radius

Shelf

Side
¼" thick–make 2

Cut one here

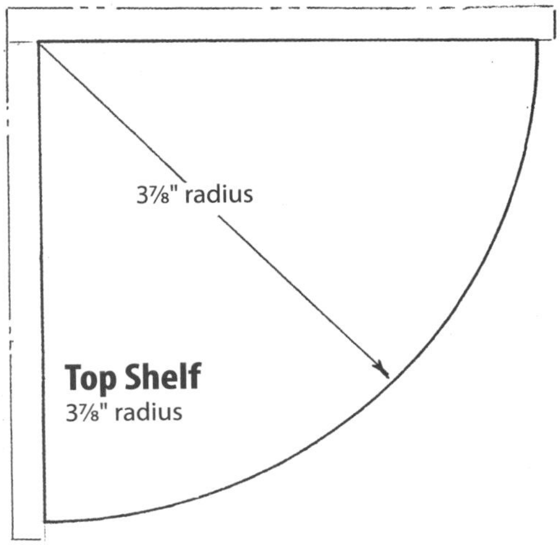

© 2009 Scroll Saw Woodworking & Crafts

Free-standing Fretwork Photo Frame

Intricate details highlight this vintage Louis XV photo frame

By Richard Preator

Picture frames always make a nice project—you can display your work and show off family photos at the same time. This classic frame also looks a lot better than the frames available at most stores today.

Start by selecting your wood for the frame. I use ³⁄₁₆"-thick wild cherry. I make two frames at one time and use nails to attach two layers together to stack cut. Choose two open fret areas inside the pattern as far apart as possible to nail the pieces together. I drill blade entry holes for the nails and cut off any protruding nails with a pair of side-cutting wire cutters. Be sure to wear safety glasses when cutting off the nails.

This photo frame, based on a 1924 pattern, looks great with any photo.

This project is in honor of our great nephew, Joshua Neusche, age 20, who died in Iraq on July 12, 2003. The finished frame will be a gift to his parents.

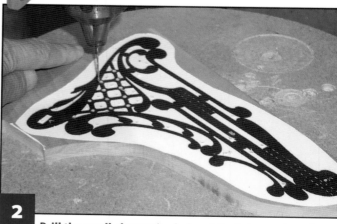

1 **Cut the backing plate.** The backing plate creates a pocket on the rear of the frame for inserting the photo. I cut the width and length to size on the table saw before attaching the pattern, but you can also cut it all on a scroll saw and square up the edges by sanding. Cut out the spacers for the back plate on the table saw as well. If you cut the spacers on the scroll saw, sand the miters to fit.

2 **Drill the small, decorative holes at the intersection of the side panels.** Use a ⁵⁄₆₄"-diameter drill bit. If you plan to cut two frames, stack two sets of side panels.

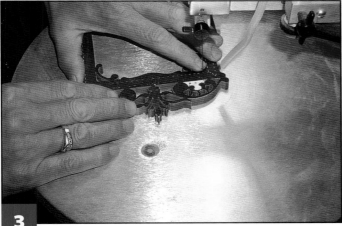

3 **Cut the photo frame face.** Cut all of the interior frets except the two frets that are nailed through. Cut the outside profile. Cut the nailed fret areas. Leave the scrap in place after cutting the first of these; it will help to keep the two parts from separating while you cut the last fret. If you make only one frame, cut the large opening for the photo last to provide added support while cutting the smaller fret areas.

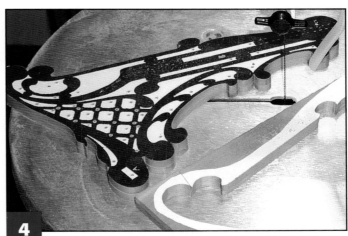

4 **Cut out the sides.** Stack cut these by nailing through two interior frets. Cut the outside profile first. Then follow the same procedure you used to cut out the photo frame face (see Step 3). If you are making two frames, you will have to cut two sets of sides.

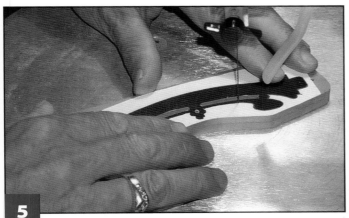

5 **Cut out the cross brace.** Since cherry burns easily, slow your saw down, let the blade do its work, and change blades often. Attach the pieces of stock with double-sided tape to make two frames.

6 **Glue up the frame face, spacers, and backing plate.** First, sand all the pieces with progressively finer grits of sandpaper up to 220-grit. Start assembling the frame by gluing the spacers to the back of the frame face. Then, glue the backing plate onto those spacers.

7 **Test fit your sidepieces and cross brace.** During my test fit, the tenon on the cross brace was a little too tight, so I use a small flat file to even out the high spots in the mating mortise.

8 **Glue the sidepieces and cross brace to the frame face.** Small spring clamps work best. You can use a minimal amount of glue on the joints since the mortise and tenon construction gives the frame a lot of strength. Finish the frame with gloss polyurethane.

Cross Brace

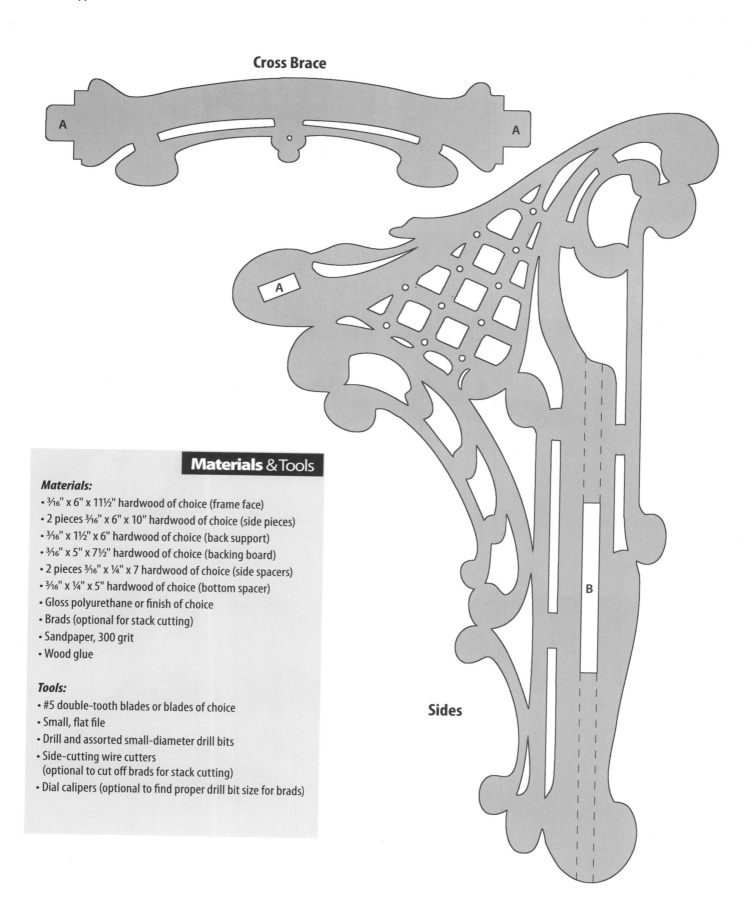

Materials & Tools

Materials:
- $\frac{3}{16}$" x 6" x $11\frac{1}{2}$" hardwood of choice (frame face)
- 2 pieces $\frac{3}{16}$" x 6" x 10" hardwood of choice (side pieces)
- $\frac{3}{16}$" x $1\frac{1}{2}$" x 6" hardwood of choice (back support)
- $\frac{3}{16}$" x 5" x $7\frac{1}{2}$" hardwood of choice (backing board)
- 2 pieces $\frac{3}{16}$" x $\frac{1}{4}$" x 7 hardwood of choice (side spacers)
- $\frac{3}{16}$" x $\frac{1}{4}$" x 5" hardwood of choice (bottom spacer)
- Gloss polyurethane or finish of choice
- Brads (optional for stack cutting)
- Sandpaper, 300 grit
- Wood glue

Tools:
- #5 double-tooth blades or blades of choice
- Small, flat file
- Drill and assorted small-diameter drill bits
- Side-cutting wire cutters
  (optional to cut off brads for stack cutting)
- Dial calipers (optional to find proper drill bit size for brads)

Sides

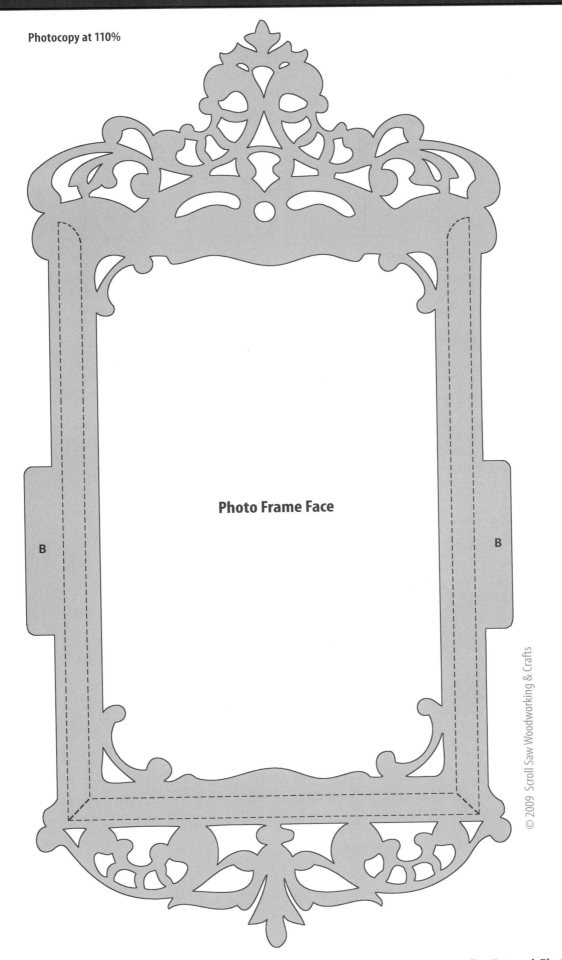

Photo Frame Face

B

B

© 2009 Scroll Saw Woodworking & Crafts

Photocopy at 110%

Spacers

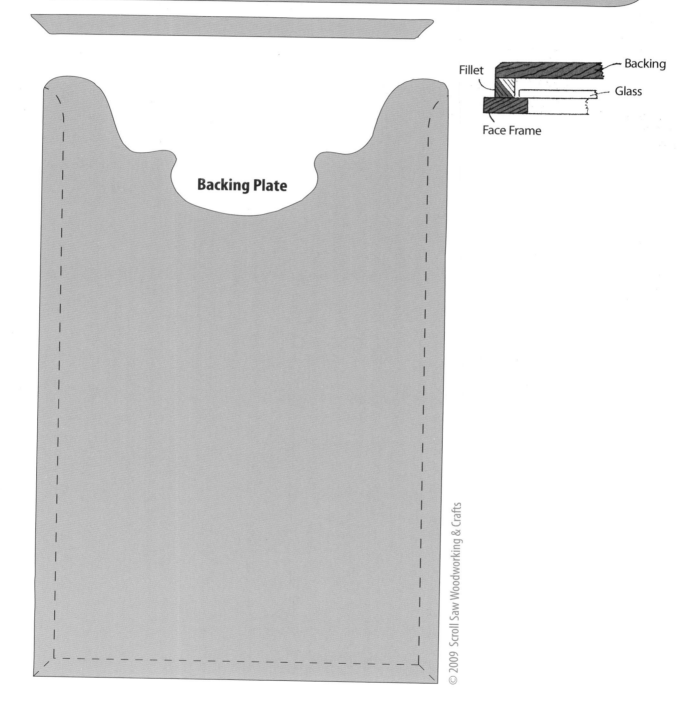

Backing Plate

Fillet

Backing

Glass

Face Frame

Fish Fretwork

A design suitable for a child's room or a beach cottage

By Ellen Brown

The curves of the seawood contrast nicely with the sleek lines of the fish, giving the project great character.

The fun design makes a unique addition to a child's room or beach cottage. Cut the pattern from thin plywood for a creative alternative to the rolled aquarium backing.

Materials & Tools

Materials:
- ¾" x 7" x 7" wood of choice
- Masking tape
- Temporary bond spray adhesive
- Assorted grits of sandpaper
- Danish oil, tung oil, or finish of choice
- Lint-free cloth
- Wood glue
- Hanger for wall mounting (optional)

Tools:
- #5 reverse-tooth blades or blades of choice
- Drill or drill press with bits to match sizes of blades
- Sander of choice or sanding block
- Paintbrush for applying finish

Photocopy at 100%

Persian-style Mirror Frame

Repeating design highlights your scrolling skills

By Richard Preator
Cut by Dale Helgerson

This exotic design was originally intended as a mirror frame, but lends itself nicely to other applications as well. Try enlarging or reducing the pattern and cutting a variety of sizes to create a striking display. Size the pattern for a 3"-diameter clock insert, or enlarge it for a special portrait or photo.

The intricacy of the design makes this a challenging project for beginners. Because it is a repeating pattern, inconsistencies in cutting will be obvious. Cut a small portion from scrap wood first to get a feel for the design. Once you're comfortable with cutting the basic shapes, you'll find it easier to repeat the cuts with confidence and consistency.

The delicate fretwork can be fragile. For a novice scroller, I suggest using Baltic birch plywood because the plywood is stronger than most other woods. Stack cutting also adds support to the delicate areas.

If you use hardwoods, I recommend cutting the main piece from a light hardwood, such as maple or birch, and the overlay from a dark hardwood, such as mahogany or walnut. You could also stain or dye plywood to simulate these colors.

Use caution when cutting the center circle. For a perfectly round circle, cut away from the line and sand up to it. Cut the mirrored acrylic to fit into the center circle of the main piece. The center circle of the overlay is slightly smaller and will neatly hide the joint.

Use the biggest bit you can for the blade entry holes. I use a ³⁄₃₂"-diameter drill bit to drill out the decorative circles on the overlay. Sand the pieces lightly after cutting to remove any burrs.

Apply your finish of choice. To assemble the frame, use epoxy to glue the mirrored acrylic into the main piece. Then, use cyanoacrylate (CA) glue to attach the overlay. Attach your hanger of choice and remember to sign your work.

Alter the design to make a striking wall clock by leaving the overlay solid and drilling a hole through the center to accommodate a clock movement.

Materials & Tools

Materials:
- ¼"-½" x 14" x 14" plywood or wood of choice (main piece)
- ⅛"-¼" x 7" x 7" plywood or contrasting wood of choice (overlay)
- 5"-diameter piece of mirrored acrylic
- Dye, stain, or finish of choice
- Sandpaper, 220 grit
- Epoxy
- Cyanoacrylate (CA) glue

Tools:
- #2 reverse-tooth blades or blades of choice
- Drill with ¹⁄₁₆" and ³⁄₃₂"-diameter drill bits
- Rags or brushes to apply finish

Photocopy at 100%

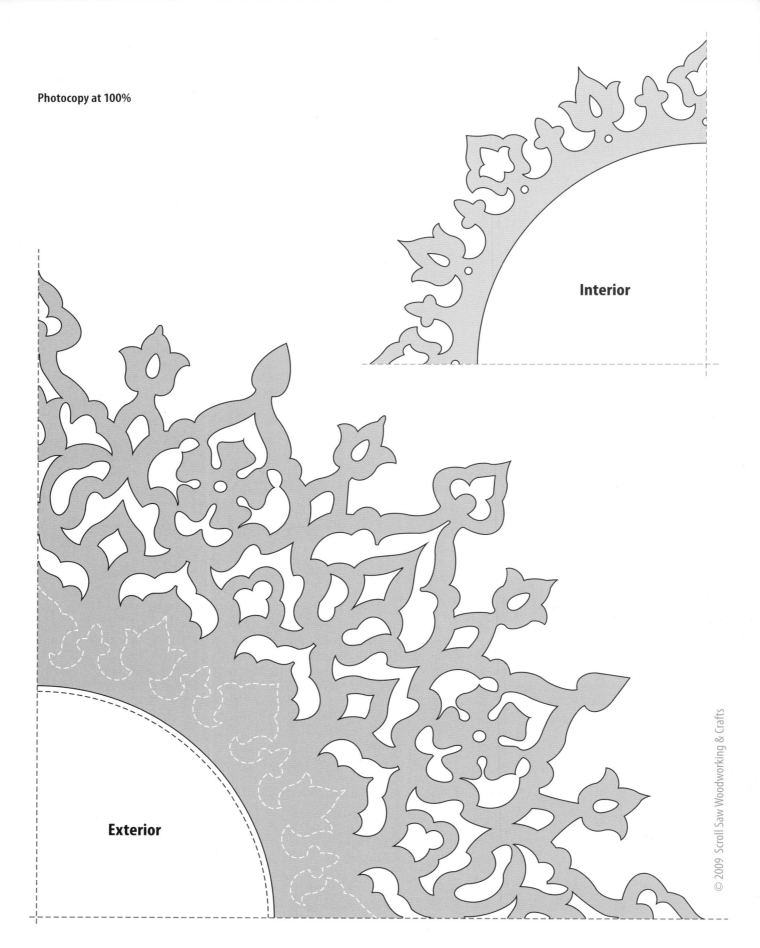

Interior

Exterior

Elegant Fretwork

Classic Roman clock face is easy to scroll

By Sue Mey

The fretwork portion of this project, with roman numerals and scrolls, is simple enough for a beginner to achieve good results. Paired with a simple backing board of a contrasting color, it makes a striking wall clock. The overlay can also be used to replace a store bought mechanism on more complex projects.

I use walnut stain to darken the overlay, but a dark hardwood can be used instead. Maple, beech, and light oak are all good choices for the backing.

Cut the blanks to the size listed in the materials list, then sand with 150-grit sandpaper. Sand the wood again with 320-grit sandpaper. This reduces the amount of hand sanding you need to do later; you run the risk of breaking the fragile parts of the overlay if you wait to sand after cutting.

I find I have better control if I stack cut the clock face. This provides support for the fragile areas and allows me to make several projects at once. Cover the surface of the workpiece with masking tape to allow for easy removal of the pattern after cutting. Apply the pattern to the taped surface. Use a compass to draw an 8"-diameter circle on the backing piece. Mark the center position using a punch and mallet.

Cutting and Sanding the Clock

1 **Drill the blade entry holes and cut the frets.** Use a ⅛"-diameter bit where space allows and a ¹⁄₁₆"-diameter bit for tight areas. Remove any burrs from the back by scraping with the grain of the wood. Use a #3 blade and reduce the speed when cutting fragile parts.

2 **Sand the edges of the work pieces.** After all frets are cut, cut the perimeter on the overlay and backing board with a #9 blade. Cut outside the line and use a disc sander to sand up to the pattern lines. Turn the work pieces slowly and evenly against the disc. You can also cut the circles with the scroll saw if you prefer.

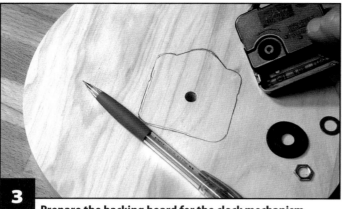

3 **Prepare the backing board for the clock mechanism.** Drill the center hole for the quartz movement shaft, using the corresponding bit for your shaft diameter. Place the movement in position on the rear of the backing board, and draw the outline with a sharp pencil.

4 **Finish shaping the backing board.** Carve an opening for the quartz movement. Create the recess to the proper depth so the shaft will protrude enough in the front. Use carving tools or a router to create the recess. Using a router and a round-over bit, round over the front edge of the backing board.

Finishing the Clock

5 **Remove the pattern and masking tape.** Separate the plywood layers by inserting your blade of choice between the two pieces and prying them apart. Sand the pieces by hand with 320-grit sandpaper. Switch to 500-grit sandpaper to get a smooth finish. Be careful not to catch and break any fragile pieces. Remove all of the sanding dust.

6 **Apply your finish.** Use a small paintbrush to apply deep-penetrating furniture wax liquid or Danish oil to the backing piece. Apply walnut stain to the front and side surfaces of the face. A small brush makes it easy to reach all the inside surfaces of the fretwork. Allow the pieces to dry, and wipe all of the surfaces with a dry, lint-free cloth.

7 **Glue up the clock.** Line up the clock face with the recess on the back. Apply small beads of wood glue to the back of the clock face piece. Position it on the backing board, and clamp it in place. Remove any glue squeeze-out with a toothpick. When dry, apply several thin coats of clear spray varnish.

8 **Finish assembling the clock.** Attach a sawtooth hanger to the back. Place the quartz movement in position, and tighten the nut in the front. Insert the clock hands onto the shaft: first the hour, then the minute, and finally the second hand. Insert a battery, and set the correct time.

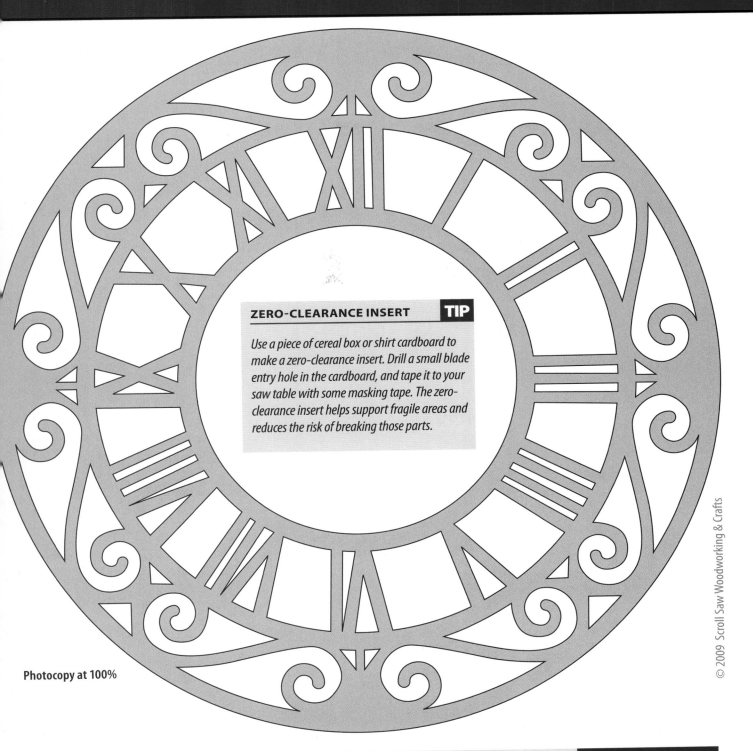

ZERO-CLEARANCE INSERT `TIP`

Use a piece of cereal box or shirt cardboard to make a zero-clearance insert. Drill a small blade entry hole in the cardboard, and tape it to your saw table with some masking tape. The zero-clearance insert helps support fragile areas and reduces the risk of breaking those parts.

Photocopy at 100%

Materials & Tools

Materials:
- 1" x 9" x 9" light-colored hardwood of choice (backing)
- ⅛" x 8" x 8" Baltic birch plywood or hardwood of choice (overlay)
- Masking tape
- Spray adhesive
- Thin, double-sided tape (optional)
- Sandpaper, assorted grits
- Wood stain, walnut (optional)
- Deep-penetrating furniture wax liquid or Danish oil
- Lint-free cloth
- Wood glue
- Clear spray varnish
- Sawtooth hanger
- Quartz movement and hands

Tools:
- #3 and #9 reverse-tooth blades or blades of choice
- Drill press with 1/16"-, ⅛"- and 5/16"-diameter bits (size of the larger bit may vary to match the shaft diameter of quartz movement)
- Disc sander and palm sander
- Router with round-over bit
- Punch and mallet
- Sharp pencil
- Clamps, assorted sizes
- Assorted paintbrushes of choice to apply the finish

156

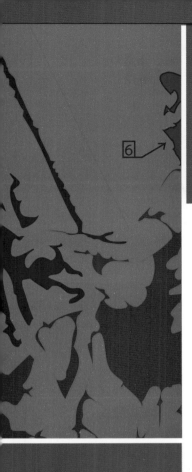

Portraits

Scroll saw portraits are projects created from photos. A photo is first manipulated in a computer program to create a pattern that can be sawn. Then, the cutting process involves relatively detailed cutting to capture the realism of the photo. The finished portrait is placed against a black or dark background to show all of the details. Because of their often personal nature, these projects make excellent keepsake gifts.

Creating Portraits in Wood

By Gary Browning

Most of us have several photographs that we proudly display in our homes or carry in our wallet to show off at a moment's notice. Gary Browning developed a way to turn those cherished photos into wooden keepsakes and pioneered the art of scroll saw portraits.

Gary is passionate about creating patterns from photographs. He is the founder of an online club for scroll saw portrait artists. The club's latest project, "Portrait Freedom," is set up to honor the families of the fallen heroes of Operations Iraqi Freedom and Enduring Freedom with a custom designed and hand-crafted wooden portrait of their loved one.

The key to creating a portrait pattern is to start with a high-quality photograph that is in focus. Close-up photos allow you to capture the details more accurately. When designing your own patterns, you can combine elements from several different pictures to capture the scene you want to portray.

There are several different software programs available that will help you create a scroll saw pattern from a photograph. You can start with a digital photograph or use a scanner to convert conventional photos to a digital format. To learn more about creating patterns from photographs, check out Gary's book *Scroll Saw Portraits*.

In their first group project, Gary's online scroll saw club joined together to create wooden portraits for the family members of the astronauts of the space shuttle Columbia.

Photos:

- In focus
- Subject not torn or faded
- Solid background
- Good highlights
- Good shadows
- Lots of close-up detail
  (Lesser-quality photos can be used, but
  making patterns from them will require
  some extra time and effort)

Computer Software:

- Look for a program that can manipulate
  photographs. You want to be able to
  enlarge or reduce a photo to suit
  your needs.
- You want to be able to lighten or darken
  the photograph with contrast and
  brightness settings. This is important in the
  silhouetting process.
- You want to be able to turn a color
  photograph into a black-and-white
  photograph, commonly called grayscale.
- You need to be able to crop the photo to
  cut out unwanted background elements.
- You may want a program that will allow
  you to piece together elements from
  many photos.

The club is honoring
the fallen soldiers of
Operation Iraqi Freedom
and Operation Enduring
Freedom by presenting
family members with
portraits of their loved ones.

Gary began designing
scroll saw portraits
to preserve cherished
family photos.

Firefighters and Flag at Ground Zero

Capture America's indomitable spirit

By Gary Browning

In a poignant display of America's indomitable spirit, three firefighters raised the American Flag amidst the ashes and rubble of Ground Zero, the site where the World Trade Center towers stood prior to the September 11 terrorist attack. Gary Browning, noted Fox Chapel Publishing author, scrolled a version of that famous photo. His cutting instructions follow.

HANDLING MISTAKES — **TIP**

Making mistakes—and I make my share of them—is never welcomed, but it is always inevitable. Rather than getting discouraged, though, I figure out how I can prevent the mistake from happening again. "Learn from your mistakes" is probably the best piece of advice I can give that will improve your overall scrolling enjoyment.

I can also share with you some tips specific to this type of portrait scrolling. When you break a piece, keep your bearings and stay focused on the remainder of the project. If it's a very small piece that breaks, just take some wood glue and re-attach it. Let the piece dry before continuing. But you could also do what I do: put the piece aside and remember where it went. At the end of cutting, set the piece up. Step back and try to find where the piece broke. If it doesn't stand out to you, then it will not stand out to anyone else. Find the area that is broken and just smooth it over by cutting the jagged edges with your scroll saw. If the wood cracks or splinters beyond repair, you can always fill the damaged areas with wood putty, sand it off and paint the surface with a light-colored or a textured paint.

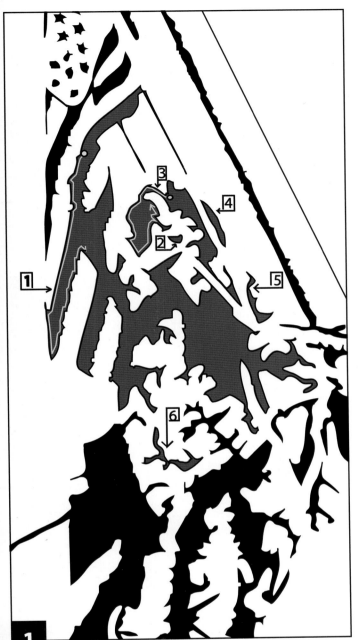

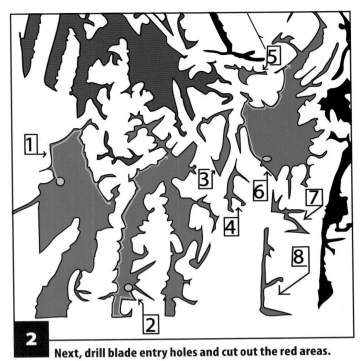

2 Next, drill blade entry holes and cut out the red areas.

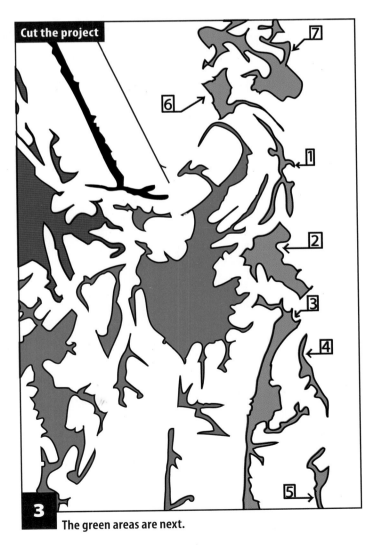

Cut the project

3 The green areas are next.

1 **Prepare and drill.** After attaching the pattern with temporary bond spray adhesive, drill the blade entry holes. Start with the blue areas and cut in the order indicated. The cutting order for this project reflects my general philosophy about cutting these types of projects: start in one area close to the center of the pattern and work one piece at a time toward the outside of the wood. By cutting this way, the cut pieces that are left in the middle of the piece of wood are the fragile parts and the pieces to be cut toward the end of the project are still supported by the strongest part of the wood. If you cut from the outside and work toward the center of the piece of wood, the vibration and blade stress could lift up the wood and cause breakage of the thin anchor points of the pattern.

For this step, as well as for Steps 2 and 5, suggested blade entry holes and cutting directions are indicated in yellow. If there are no yellow lines, the cutting direction is not important.

Next, drill blade entry holes and cut out the red areas.

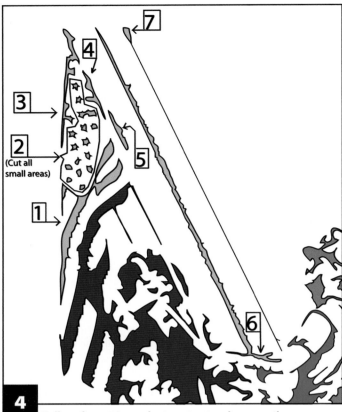

4 Follow the cutting order to cut out and remove the yellow areas.

5 Finish by cutting out the brown areas.

STACK CUTTING CREATES SUPPORT — TIP

Stack cutting two or three pieces not only speeds up production, but it also allows extra support for those very fragile areas on the bottom. Additionally, it offers you a better chance of producing at least one piece with minimal mistakes.

THINK AHEAD WHEN YOU CUT — TIP

Be smart and think ahead of the next few cuts so you don't run into an area that you should have done differently. If it's too late and you are forced to cut an area that will be a very fragile cut, don't force the blade. Feed the wood very slowly and let the blade do the cutting.

Materials & Tools

Materials:
- ¼" or ⅛" birch or oak plywood
- Temporary bond spray adhesive
- Polyurethane spray or varnish
- Sandpaper, 150 grit
- Black felt for the background
- Black mat, 11" x 14"
- Hot glue gun
- Frame of choice, 11" x 14"

Tools:
- #2 reverse-tooth blade or #2 or #3 spiral blades
- Drill with ⅟₁₆"-diameter bit

Photocopy at 100%

Scroll the Most Famous Scene of World War II

Victorious marines raise the flag at Iwo Jima

By Gary Browning

During World War II, one of the most intense and closely fought battles took place on the tiny, sulfurous island of Iwo Jima. Located only about 650 miles from Tokyo, Iwo Jima was important to both the Japanese and the United States. The Japanese considered Iwo Jima part of their home soil. It was administered by the Tokyo metropolitan government and considered part of Japan. In addition, in Japan's 5,000-year history, no foreign army had ever set foot on Japanese soil.

The United States wanted Iwo Jima because of its strategic location midway between Japan and American bomber bases in the Marianas. One-hundred thousand men battled on the tiny, eight-square-mile island for over a month. Twenty thousand Japanese soldiers were hidden underground in a sophisticated, reinforced tunnel system that crisscrossed the entire island. More than 6,800 American marines died at Iwo Jima. American forces captured Iwo Jima on February 23, 1945.

The portrait of the victorious Easy Company raising the flag atop Mt. Suribachi on Iwo Jima was captured immediately following the victory.

On the 50th anniversary of the historic flag raising, the National Iwo Jima Memorial Monument near Hartford, Connecticut was dedicated to all of the Americans who died at Iwo Jima. The memorial also features an eternal flame that burns 365 days a year, 24 hours a day, as a reminder of the sacrifices made by all those who defended freedom during World War II.

1 **Cut the blue sections.** Start with the blue shaded areas first (in any order), and then cut out the red shaded area in the direction indicated.

2 **Cut the green sections.** The next weakest points to be cut carefully will be to the left of the red-shaded pattern as pictured. The green shade is next, starting from top to bottom. Notice the blade entry hole and black directional line in the green shade that represents the recommended path to follow. You can see that I always take my first cut close to the edge of the previous piece that was cut out already. The idea is to take these cuts first so that the strength of the wood is with you to the end of the cut. If I chose to follow a counterclockwise path, it may indeed work, but there is a chance that when you make the turn where the more fragile area is, the saw may vibrate it and break it.

3 **Cut the orange sections.** In this picture, you will notice all of the black represents cut-out areas to this point. The orange-shaded areas have yet to be cut out. The blue arrows just show you that it is to your benefit to start at the already cut-out areas and hit the next closest cuts, working away from the weak wood.

4

Continue cutting. In this picture, you will notice the small blue piece should be cut out before the red area. This is a good example of using the wood's strength to your advantage. If you cut the blue piece out after the red, there is a good chance you will run into a broken piece due to vibration on the fragile piece.

This pattern has a lot of little pieces that hardly seem worth the effort to thread the blade through the blade entry hole. I personally find it necessary to make these cuts and efforts. In making a pattern from a photo, there is a great loss of detail and small pieces, such as on this pattern, but remember, there is sometimes more to the pattern. It makes your mind fill in missing details or visualize what the piece represents. It could be a small rock, a piece of vegetation, or a piece of twisted metal. The small pieces on their own are meaningless, but when they are all incorporated into the pattern, it gives a more pleasing appearance.

Photocopy at 100%

© 2009 Scroll Saw Woodworking & Crafts

Lighthouse Silhouette

Classic nautical design is a great beginner's project

By Robin Arnold

Ohio and lighthouses may seem an unlikely couple, but along the north coast of the state, which borders Lake Erie, several can still be found. One of the most popular is the Marblehead (OH) Lighthouse—which is the subject of this project.

I prefer using ½" hardwoods, usually white ash or red or white oak, but a variety of woods (including plywood) can be used. The thickness of the project is also a personal choice, although I wouldn't use hardwoods any thinner than ½" or thicker than 1".

Step 1: Sand your blank. Start with 120-grit sandpaper. Wipe off the blank with a rag before moving to 180-grit sandpaper—if 120-grit residue is left on your project when you move up to 180-grit, it can scratch the wood. Wipe off the wood again, and apply the pattern using a temporary bond spray adhesive.

Step 2: Drill all blade entry holes.

Step 3: Cut out the pieces. Start on the inside with the more delicate interior cuts, and work your way out.

Step 4: Give the piece a final sanding with 220-grit sandpaper.

Step 5: Apply your finish of choice. I use an oil finish. This gives the lighthouse a beautiful satin-smooth finish. Place a saw-tooth hanger on the back of the project and hang it as desired.

Materials & Tools

Materials:
- ½" – ¾" x 8½" x 10½" wood of choice
  Note: this leaves extra space around the piece to cut with the scroll saw. If you have access to a table saw the piece can be cut to the finished dimensions of 7⁹⁄₁₆" x 9⁹⁄₁₆"
- Sandpaper, 120, 180, and 220 grits
- Temporary bond spray adhesive
- Oil finish of choice
- Saw-tooth hanger

Tools:
- Blades of choice for ½" hardwood (I use a #5 reverse-tooth blade for the entire project)
- Drill press with small-diameter drill bit

Photocopy at 105%

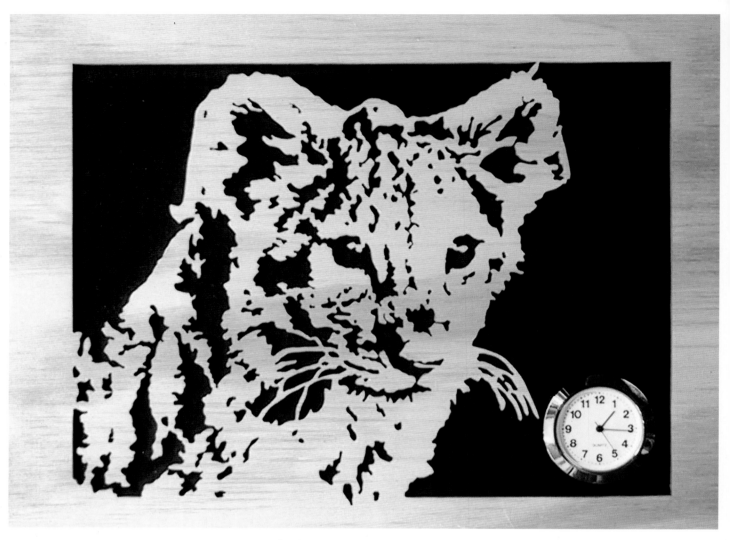

Lion Cub Portrait

A 'roaring' project all the way from South Africa

By Sue Mey

The lion is one of South Africa's "Big 5" animals, together with the elephant, leopard, buffalo, and rhinoceros. There is nothing more adorable than a baby animal, especially a lion cub, with its erect ears, huge paws, and whimpering, snarling little cries for food and attention. This project will be popular with the young... and the not so young. How can you not love that face?

Step 1: Prepare the wood and pattern. Using the palm sander, sand the wood before applying the pattern. This reduces the amount of hand sanding to be done later as well as the risk of breaking fragile pieces when sanding after cutting. Photocopy the pattern and attach it to the wood, using temporary bond spray adhesive.

Step 2: Drill the blade entry holes. Use the ⅛"-diameter bit. Carefully drill the holes in the small areas using the ¹⁄₁₆"-diameter bit. Remove burrs created by drilling the holes—use a scraper blade along the grain of the work piece at a slight angle or sandpaper.

Step 3: Cut out the pattern. Using the #2 or #3 reverse blade, thread the blade through the blade entry holes and cut off all the black areas on the pattern. Start with the inside areas and finish with the straight cuts that form the inside frame off the portrait. Slow down the speed of your saw when cutting fragile parts, such as the eyes and whiskers, and use a zero-clearance insert to reduce the risk of breaking these parts.

Step 4: Sand the portrait. Remove the pattern and sand the work piece front and back by hand with a sanding block. Use 150-grit, 320-grit, then 500-grit sandpaper to get a smooth finish. Be careful not to catch and break any fragile pieces—take special care around the whiskers. I prefer to use a three-finger sized piece of sandpaper without a sanding block, as one has more sensitivity for the pressure required when using one's hand.

Step 5: Square the four edges of both the portrait and the backing. Use the disc sander. The two pieces can be done separately and dry-fitted to ensure the two work pieces line up nicely. Alternatively, attach the portrait to the backing with thin double-sided tape or hot glue on the four corners before straight-sanding the edges. Detach the two pieces immediately afterward, as the tape becomes more sticky and difficult to remove if you leave it for a day or two. Remove all sanding dust.

Step 6: Prepare the backing. If MDF is used for a backing, spray the front, back, and edges with three thin coats of flat black spray paint, allowing it to dry completely between coats. If plywood is used for the backing, cut an 8" x 10" piece of black matting board. Apply wood glue to the back of the matting board and place on top of the plywood backing. Working fast, apply wood glue to the back of the portrait. Only small beads of glue are needed near the edges and on the fragile pieces like the whiskers—too much glue will seep

out once clamped. Place the portrait on top of the matting board and "square up" the stack on a flat surface. Clamp the corners and along the frame sides. Attach at least two clamps on the face of the cub and one on the whiskers. If glue seepage occurs, wait until the glue starts to thicken before removing excess glue in a small area at a time, using a toothpick. For the MDF backing, apply the portrait directly to the painted backing as described above.

Step 7: Drill the hole for the clock. Once the glue has dried, remove clamps. Drill the hole for the clock insert to the correct depth, using the drill press and Forstner bit. Remove any dust.

Step 8: Sealing the portrait. Apply several thin coats of clear spray varnish, allowing the project to dry thoroughly between coats. Attach the saw-tooth hanger and insert the clock. Now the cub is able to tell when it is time for its next feed!

Materials & Tools

Materials:

- ¼" x 8" x 10" Baltic birch plywood or plywood of choice
- ¾" x 8" x 10" Baltic birch plywood/plywood of choice or MDF for backing
- Black matting board or flat black spray paint
- Sandpaper, assorted grits
- Temporary bond spray adhesive
- Wood glue
- Packing tape
- Clear spray varnish
- Saw-tooth hanger
- If you are adding a clock to the project, you also need a 1⅜" clock insert and a drill press with a 1⅜" Forstner bit.

Tools:

- #2 or #3 reverse-tooth blade
- Drill press or drill with ⅛"- and ¹⁄₁₆"-diameter bits
- Disc sander, palm sander, sanding block
- Clamps

Photocopy at 200%

© 2009 Scroll Saw Woodworking & Crafts

The crosshairs show the placement of the clock hole on the backerboard. Add a border of your choice.

Materials Other Than Wood

As you will see in this section, scroll saw projects don't have to be limited to wood. You can scroll Corian, paper, acrylic, coins, and a variety of other things on the scroll saw and end up with some amazing results. Just be sure to use any proper precautions based on the material you choose.

Holiday Ornaments from Throwaway Items

Save money on materials the Jim Gress way

By Mark Weinstein

It has been said no two snowflakes are alike, and that's also the case when it comes to Christmas tree ornaments Jim Gress scrolls. The first ornaments he created on his Shopsmith in 1997 were wooden. He has branched out, so to speak, by scrolling ornaments from at least 18 other materials. Every December, Jim and his wife, Margaret, select an 11'-tall Douglas fir and decorate it with white lights, maroon red ribbon, and 250 ornaments he has made.

He has used trial and error to determine which blade works best with various materials. "I've snapped and broken a lot of blades over the years, but you learn from it," Jim says. Among materials he has scrolled into ornaments are Formica, Corian, compact disks, leather, paper, and starched cloth. He wraps clear packaging tape around the top and bottom of the piece to be scrolled because this keeps the blade lubricated and useful longer.

Jim uses #2 and #5 scroll saw blades. "I have a pretty good idea now that a #5 blade will work with anything in the ornament line except if it's an item that is real thin or delicate, with scroll saw cuts close together," he says.

He buys most of the patterns but has made some, including one of his church he scrolled from copper. Retired from his floor covering business, Jim scrolls his remaining materials, buys others, and obtains some from merchants' scrap bins. Once, Jim was given a 5' x 12' sheet of Formica. He's going to surprise the donor by making ornaments for her from the material.

Jim's woodshop is in the family's barn, several hundred feet from the house. He often walks to the house, to show Margaret his latest creations.

"Sometimes she laughs, sometimes she shakes her head," Jim says.

"Or I say, 'What's next?'" she adds.

Jim and Margaret take parts of two days to decorate their tree, which is up until Jan. 2. Some of the ornaments he has donated to his church have been auctioned off for as much as $100 to $120.

He has sold others through his WOOD-N-THINGS business. Jim stack cuts most of his ornaments, so they are sandwiched between plywood. Among the ornaments he sells are the plywood versions left unfinished for the buyer.

"I have found some new materials I want to work with like window screening and detergent bottles that are bright orange, blue and yellow," Jim says.

Leftovers in everyday life become objects of delight.

Making Non-Wood Ornaments

I enjoy using my imagination to create all of my different ornaments. Hopefully, you'll be inspired to try cutting ornaments from whatever materials strike your fancy. To get you started, if you've never cut anything but wood, I've put together the following bits of advice. The blade used is in parentheses after the ornament title.

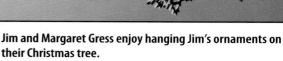

Jim and Margaret Gress enjoy hanging Jim's ornaments on their Christmas tree.

1: Tongue depressor snowflake (#2 blade). Stack cut this one, as I do for many of these other ornaments.

2, 15: Copper Snowflake and Pennsylvania Dutch hex sign (#5 blade). You'll find copper suitable for ornaments at your local craft store. The copper should be 1/32" thick. Sandwich the copper between plywood to cut so it doesn't bend. Polish the copper with metal cleaner.

3: Scrap wood 1/4" thick with photo frame insert of Max the schnauzer (#2 blade). Be sure to drill the center piece with a Forstner bit first for the frame and picture.

4: Formica angel on plywood (#5 blade). There are eight pieces to this angel and some of the cuts are delicate, so don't stray off your lines. The Formica should be 1/16" thick.

5: CD frame for Formica grand piano (#5 blade). You'll need to cut each piece separately and make sure the piano fits in the CD frame. Spray paint the piano black. The Formica should be 1/16" thick.

6: Pine 3-D apple (#5 blade). You will have to relief cut this by setting your saw table at three degrees, left side down. The pine should be 3/4" thick. Make your cuts in a counterclockwise direction. Then, pop out the cuts into place and paint the apple.

7: Corian sledding bear (#5 blade). I used Corian, stack cut between plywood, to create three ornaments from one cut. The Corian should be 1/4" thick and should be cut slowly because it is quite dense.

8: Leather buffalo (#5 blade). Leather makes a nice ornament. I used 1/4"-thick leather.

9: Indoor-outdoor carpet summer snowflake (#5 blade). Stack cut using plywood. I used approximately 1/4"-thick needle-punched carpet.

10, 12: Lucite snowflake, violin, and trumpet (#5 blade). For me, Lucite is the most challenging material to cut. As soon as you saw it, it melts back together. So I stack cut it and then put masking tape between the layers to keep them separate. When I take the tape off, I can glue the different layers together. What's nice about Lucite is, when the light shines through it, it adds new color. The Lucite and plywood should each be 1/8" thick.

11: Lucite Christmas tree with multicolored balls on plywood backing (#5 blade). Drill small holes into the Lucite, then place the plywood beneath it and through the holes, mark with a pencil where to apply the different colors of paint. The Lucite and plywood should each be 1/8" thick.

13: Copper on plywood deer (#5 blade). Polish the copper first and sandwich it between plywood. The copper should be 1/32" thick.

14: StarVinyl tile, like flooring in supermarkets (#5 blade). This one doesn't need to be stack cut, but be sure to drill your starter hole. The vinyl should be 1/8" thick.

Beyond Bathrooms and Countertops

Discover the secrets and wonders of Corian scrolling with this versatile and durable Floral Welcome Trivet.

Story and photography by Mike Randazzo
Pattern design and scrolling by Jim Carroll

It was a muggy June afternoon when I spied Jim Carroll's crafts stand at the last Stevens, Pennsylvania, scroll saw picnic. My face and neck ruddy from the beating sun, I sought refuge under Jim's awning. It was there that I discovered the curious Southwestern scenes, multi-layered angelfish, and other delightful Corian creations that were attracting the gaze of so many scrollers.

"Corian is very pleasant to scroll, and in some ways easier to work with than some woods because there are no grains to worry about," he explained to me as a scroller from the Mid-West marveled at a sleek Cobalt dolphin with Everest White inlay. "'Anything you can do with wood, you can do with Corian,' is what I always tell scrollers," Carroll elaborated.

Pattern Preparation and Cutting:

First, place a layer of duct tape on the topside of the Corian. Duct tape helps to keep the material cool while cutting. It also helps to keep the dust particles from being drawn back down into the kerf and fusing the material back together, which makes the pieces difficult to separate.

Materials & Tools

Materials:
- ¼"–½" by 8" by 10" piece of Corian
- #5 and #7 skip-tooth precision ground blade
- Wet/dry sandpaper, 300, 600, 800, 1200, and 2400 grit
- Duct, masking, or packaging tape
- Cabinet protective dots (optional)
- Leather strapping, about 18" long (optional)

Tools:
- Drill or drill press
- Random orbital sander or hand sander
- ¹⁄₁₆"-diameter or smaller drill bits
- Router with a ½" round-over bit (optional)
- Hot glue gun or cyanoacrylate glue (optional)
- Rotary polishing tool with diamond-tipped bit (optional)

"Scrollers can use masking tape or clear packaging tape, but I have found duct tape works better," Carroll said.

Next, apply a fairly heavy coat of repositional spray glue to the pattern. Immediately apply the pattern to the duct tape. Press the pattern down firmly and let it set for about five minutes. Lastly, drill your 1/16" blade entry holes into the inside cut sections.

Corian is fragile when cut thin. If you drop a piece that has been cut, chances are it'll break. Cut the outside perimeter of the project first. When sawing the more ornate parts of the floral pattern, Jim recommends scrolling the smaller sections first, then the larger pieces.

"If you are cutting two sections that are going to cut a very thin wall in between them, try to be mindful that you should leave that wall a little thicker than maybe you normally would with a piece of wood," he noted.

When cutting Corian, it's important to keep a fairly constant level of pressure, but there is no need to push hard. Cutting at a slower speed is recommended. For example, Carroll sets his saw speed to medium, or about 700-800 strokes per minute.

"Let the blade do the work for you. Keep your pressure constant, but you don't have to push heavily into the blade," the scroller advised. Jim uses a #7 skip-tooth precision ground blade for 80 to 90% of his work. He relies on a #5 blade for some of the finer fretwork. This material can be stacked up to one inch, Carroll reported, but if you plan on stack-cutting this project a #9 blade may be a wiser choice.

After all your cuts have been made, remove the duct tape and the pattern.

Finishing Touches:

While Corian sawing doesn't produce tearout-like imperfections, you may find powdery saw marks especially on the larger inside cuts. These marks can be smoothed with a rotary polishing tool outfitted with a diamond-tipped bit.

Next, you can rout the top and bottom edges with a 1/2" round-over bit, which makes for a nice finished touch, especially for selling at a craft show. "Corian is a little tougher on carbide-tipped router bits, but if you use a slow speed rate and let the router do the work, your router bits will do the job," said Carroll.

CORIAN SCROLLING	TIP

To reduce saw marks when making the inside cuts and turning tight corners, scrollers can round over the backs of their saw blades with a sharpening stone similar to the one used on band saw blades. To do this, tension the blade and run the saw at top speed. Then, rotate the stone over the back of the blade alternating from the left side to the right side. This process only takes about 10 seconds to complete on each side.

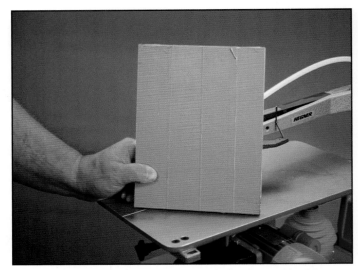

Under wraps: A single layer of duct tape applied to the topside of the Corian prevents the material from being drawn into the kerf.

Covering the bases: Apply the pattern to the duct tape immediately after gluing and let it set for about five minutes.

Drilling down: Use a 1/16" drill bit to make the blade entry holes for the Floral Welcome Trivet's inside cuts.

On the edge: When scrolling the Floral Welcome Trivet, make the outside cuts first. Take your time and use a steady feed rate.

Fun with floral frets: When sawing the ornate parts of the floral pattern, scroll the larger sections first, then the smaller pieces.

When sanding, it's best to start with 300-grit wet/dry sandpaper and progress to 2400 grit. Jim recommends the following sequence: 300, 600, 800, 1200, 2400. Corian sanding is basically a two-step process that can be completed in less than 10 minutes.

Scrollers should rinse the surface of the piece between each grit change to remove all the particles and dust from the previous grit. The 1200 and 2400 grit sanding can be done with the piece wet, and additional water can be applied during these last two steps if the surface dries out. "I have a squirt bottle with water in it and I just spray the surface as needed," Carroll noted.

Move the sander or sandpaper in a horizontal motion from left edge to right edge, then in a vertical motion top to bottom, then diagonally in both directions. Jim uses a variable speed random orbit sander set on medium, and it usually takes about one minute per grit. What's more, he

Out of orbit: Orbital sanders, like this one, produce a smoother finish on Corian because they create random sanding strokes.

advises that scrollers sand the edges too, in order to remove any routing marks.

"Sanding Corian by hand doesn't achieve quite the same finish because the sanding marks are more visible. I use the orbital sander because it creates a random pattern of strokes, which makes for a smoother finish," Carroll explained.

Mounting and Other Helpful Corian Tidbits:

The trivet can be mounted for either inside or outdoor use. For counter duty, Jim glues clear plastic stoppers, commonly found on cabinet doors, to each corner of the trivet. For outside or wall duty, drill two ⅛" holes as shown on the pattern, feed the leather strap through the front of the hole, and tie a knot in the back.

A "kinder-gentler" tearout: Saw marks can be dressed with a rotary polishing tool or removed with sandpaper and a dowel.

Local kitchen or bath contractors may be a good source for materials left over from sink cutouts. "I often flip through the Yellow Pages and find the contractors that install Corian countertops," Carroll offered. On one occasion, he even scrolled a nameplate with the contractor's logo, which won him a handful of free samples. Be advised, however, that some contractors won't part with this stock easily, if at all.

All in all, Corian is a fun way to expand your scrolling horizons, and in many ways it acts like wood. For example, when you come to a 90° corner, cut into the corner on one side and then go into the waste area and cut in from the other side, just like you would with a piece of Baltic birch.

It takes time to learn the quirks and unique personality of this alternative scrolling material. "Just go slow, take your time and practice. Take a scrap piece and cut little circles or whatever shapes you're most comfortable with. But, just get used to the feel of it and the pressure that it takes," Carroll concluded.

Reporting for Counter Duty: With plastic stoppers like those shown here, your finished trivet is ready for service in the kitchen.

More about Corian®

Corian is a registered trademark of the E.I. Du Pont de Nemours and Company, headquartered in Wilmington, Delaware. It comes in more than 80 colors, ranging from Black Pearl to Glacier White and everything in between, including such exotic shades as Kiwi, Mandarin, and Lilac.

According to the fine folks at Du Pont, the substance is an advanced blend of natural materials and pure acrylic polymers. It's manufactured as a continuous cast sheet; the sheets are pre-cut into specific lengths and shipped to distributors across the country for household and commercial use. The most popular sizes for scrolling are 9" by 12" rectangles that are ½" thick—the size that you would order for this trivet.

Optional ⅛" holes for hanging

Photocopy at 100%

Cutting Coins

A simple jig makes it easy to cut coins on your scroll saw

By Jon Ferre

The Kansas quarter is a fairly simple design and a good coin to start with.

The scroll saw can be used to cut a variety of different coins. I started cutting the scenes on state quarters because I collect coins and had made a coin map for my quarter collection. Scrolled coins also make unique jewelry.

Through trial and error, I devised a simple jig and found that cutting coins is a fun—and challenging—way to scroll away a few hours. Because the metal in quarters is not very hard, I use a #2 blade for most of the cutting. I switch to a #2/0 blade for the more detailed sections. If you plan to scroll different coins, try experimenting with blade selection to find the one that works best for you.

PLAN YOUR CUTS	**TIP**

Use caution when deciding what details to cut; I tried to cut the Great Lakes out on the Michigan coin, but the coin broke while I was cutting it.

Making the Cutting Jig

1

Lay out the cutting jig. Cut a ¾" x 2" x 2" piece of hardwood (I use oak). Determine the center, and mark it with a center punch or awl. Drill through the center with a ⅛"-diameter drill bit. This hole will be your guide hole.

2 **Create the top opening.** Drill a ¹⁵⁄₁₆"-diameter hole ⅛" deep using the guide hole as your center point. Use a Forstner bit. You want to drill the hole slightly deeper than the quarter is thick.

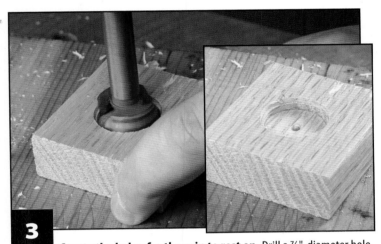

3 **Create the ledge for the coin to rest on.** Drill a ⅞"-diameter hole ⅛" deeper into the block in the center of the first hole. This will give you a ¹⁄₁₆"-wide shoulder to hold the coin. Use a Forstner bit.

4 **Create the bottom opening.** Drill a ¹⁵⁄₁₆"-diameter hole in from the opposite side. Continue drilling until you meet the ⅞"-diameter hole. Be careful not to drill so deep that you remove the shoulder. Use a Forstner bit.

State quarters offer a variety of designs for different skill levels.

MAKING TURNS · TIP

When cutting metal, do not try to spin your blade. It WILL break. You can make long, sweeping curves, but to cut a tight corner, nibble away with the scroll saw blade until the kerf is big enough for you to rotate the blade without touching either side of the cut line.

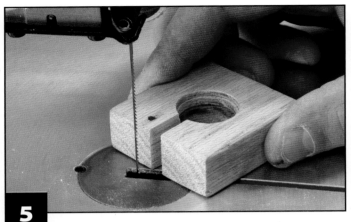

5 **Cut the expansion slot.** Cut a ¼"-wide slot through one side. This allows the holder to expand so you can get the quarter in and out easily, but still provides enough tension to grip the quarter tightly.

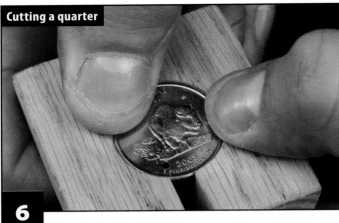

6 **Place the coin in the jig.** You may need to spread the jig a bit with a screwdriver to fit the coin in. I am using Kansas, because it is a good design for beginners to cut.

7 **Mark the location of the blade entry holes.** Use a center punch to make sure the drill bit doesn't wander. Plan to drill several holes so you can cut as many straight lines as possible—this keeps the blades from breaking as often. Drill the holes using a #60 drill bit. If you don't have a drill bit that small, you can use a ¹⁄₁₆"-diameter bit, but you'll have to use caution.

8 **Thread your blade through a hole.** Apply a drop of light sewing machine oil to the tip of your finger, and rub it on the back and sides of the blade. Don't apply too much oil, or it will puddle, collect shavings, and obscure the pattern. The oil lubricates the blade and makes it easier to cut the metal. Connect the holes with your first cut.

9 **Cut out the details.** Increase the width of the lines cut in Step 8 until you can easily rotate your blade without touching either side. Then, start to make straight cuts into the more detailed areas. Continue scrolling until you have cut all of the details you want. Use needle files to remove the burrs and to smooth out any rough spots. Smooth the curves out with the files. Then, polish the coin, using metal polish or a buffing wheel.

Materials & Tools

Materials:
- ¾" x 2" x 2" hardwood block (I use oak), cutting jig
- State quarter of choice
- Light sewing machine oil
- Metal polish (optional)

Tools:
- Center punch
- Drill
- ⅛"-diameter and #60 or ¹⁄₁₆"-diameter metal drill bit
- Forstner drill bits, ¹⁵⁄₁₆" diameter and ⅞" diameter
- Needle files
- Buffing wheel (optional)
- Screwdriver (to help put coin in jig)

Custom Note Cards

Strike a happy note with musical instruments cut in paper

By Stephen Miklos

Group several silhouettes in a frame for a striking display.

A handmade greeting card makes keeping in touch much more personal. I designed the first of these musical instrument cards for customers of my mountain dulcimer business. They were so well-received that I decided to design the full bluegrass band.

To make the cards, cut an overlay and glue it to a cardstock backing. Stack cut dozens of overlays at once out of any kind of good paper, coverstock, or cardstock. For the card itself, you can get pre-scored cardstock or fold your own. The designs work equally well in bright, contrasting colors for a vibrant effect or with subtle pastel colors with little contrast for a ghostly effect.

Start by cutting your stock to size

The overlay should be cut to 3¾" x 5". This allows a ¼" border around the overlay on a standard U.S. card size of 5½" x 4¼". The best way to do this is with a paper cutter. Cut two pieces of plywood or stiff cardboard to the same size. Sandwich the paper between the two backing pieces. I wrap mine with blue painter's tape. The blue tape is easy to peel off afterward. Apply the pattern to the top of the stack with spray glue.

PAPER CUTTING TIPS   TIP

Cutting stacks of paper is similar to stacks of wood, but there are a few things to be aware of.

1. ***Paper has very little stiffness.*** *You will need to sandwich the paper stack between two pieces of wood or stiff cardboard.*
2. ***Paper burns more easily than wood.*** *Keep the saw speed moderate, and keep the work moving so the blade doesn't rub too long in one place.*
3. ***I use a #2 crown-tooth blade for this work.*** *Anything finer is more likely to burn the paper and anything coarser can make a ragged edge. A crown-tooth design helps to keep the cut smooth throughout the stack.*
4. ***Cutting paper creates a lot of fine dust.*** *You never know what dyes and chemicals went into the paper. Always wear a dust mask when scrolling, but especially when scrolling paper.*
5. ***You can cut a fairly thick pile of paper with little trouble.*** *To keep from bogging down the saw, I usually keep my stack about ¾" or less. That produces between 50 and 200 overlays, depending on the weight of the sheets. I like to mix up different weights, colors, and textures to come up with a variety of overlays.*
6. ***Purchase paper from an office supply store, an art store, or a specialty paper store.*** *Be wary of cheap construction paper sold for kids; it starts to fade as soon as any light hits it.*

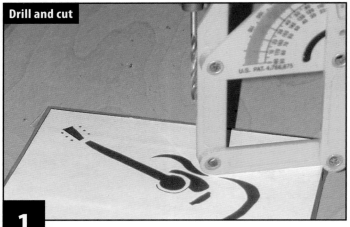

1

Drill blade entry holes for the inside cuts. For the larger openings, use a ⅛"-diameter bit. Use a ¹⁄₁₆"-diameter bit for the small openings. Be sure to drill the blade entry holes straight down through the stack. Drill the tuner buttons on the guitar, mandolin, and dulcimer with a ¹⁄₁₆"-diameter bit.

2

Cut the sound hole on the guitar. Don't use a drill bit; a perfect circle would change the style and feel of the pattern. A crisp corner where the sound hole meets the fingerboard is important. Cut all around the circle first, then head straight up the sides of the neck.

3

Cut into corners first from one side, then the other. Don't try to turn in the corner; the paper is more likely to burn than wood.

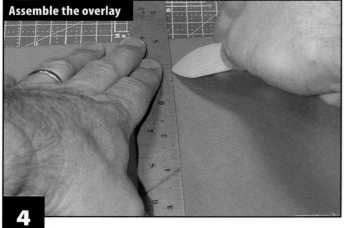

4

Assemble the cards. Cut a letter-size sheet of cardstock into two 5½" x 8½" pieces. Lightly mark a centerline to divide the sheet into two 5½" x 4¼" sections. Place a straightedge along the line, and score the fold line with the blunt end of a butter knife or the pointed end of a bone folder. This will compress the fibers of the paper, leaving a crease that will ensure a crisp fold right where you want it. The crease should be visible as an indentation on the inside of the card and as a ridge on the outside.

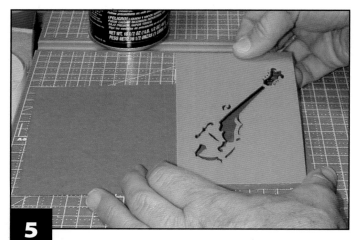

5

Adhere the overlay to the cardstock. Using a spraying rack, spray a coat of adhesive to the back of the overlay. Center the overlay on the front of the card material. Be sure the inside of the card is down, and place the overlay on the right-hand section. Then fold the card. Use the flat of the bone folder to burnish the fold and keep it flat.

Materials & Tools

Materials:
- Paper for overlays
- Cardstock for note cards
- Cardboard or plywood for stack cutting
- Spray adhesive (to adhere the pattern on the stack and the overlay on the card)

Tools:
- #2 crown-tooth blades or blades of choice
- Drill with ⅛"- and ¹⁄₁₆"-diameter drill bits
- Bone folder or butter knife
- Paper cutter
- Straightedge

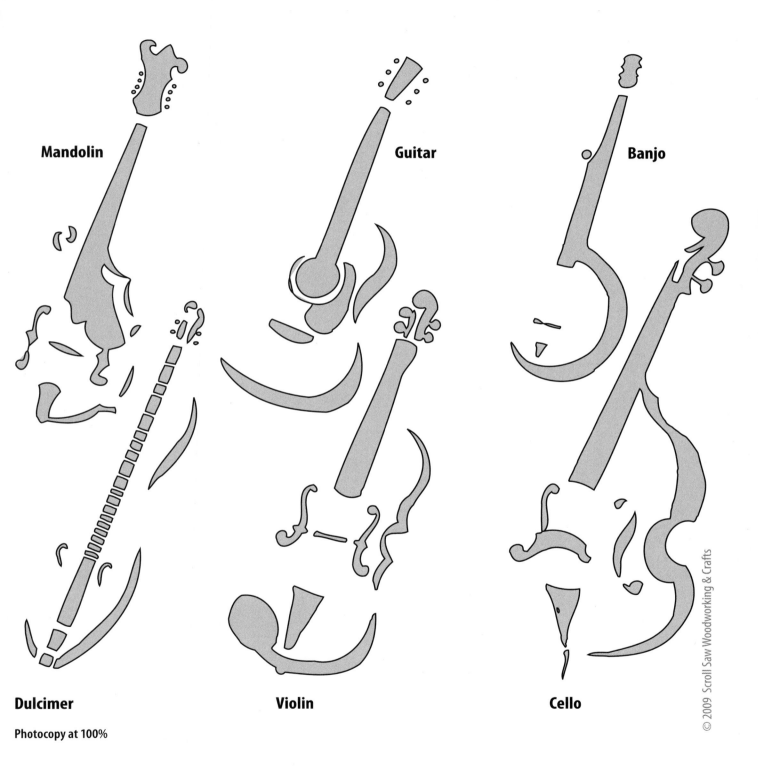

Mandolin

Guitar

Banjo

Dulcimer

Photocopy at 100%

Violin

Cello

© 2009 Scroll Saw Woodworking & Crafts

Index

Contributors

Robin Arnold
Robin, of Port Clinton, Ohio, is also a semi-professional wildlife/nature photographer.

Ellen Brown
Ellen lives in Brunswick, Maine.

Ron Brown
Ron, a resident of Lawrenceville, Ga., is a professional woodworker and trim carpenter.

Gary Browning
Gary is known for his scrolled portraits and lives in Greencastle, Pa.
www.angelfire.com/md2/creativewood/browning.htm

Jim Carroll
Jim, who lives in Pa., enjoys scrolling Corian.

Theresa Ekdom
Theresa lives in northern Michigan.

Jon Ferre
Jon lives in Sandy, Utah.

John Fleig
John lives in Sulphur, La.
www.unclejohns.com

Rick Gillespie
Rick, an accomplished woodworker, began creating intarsia pieces in 1999.

Jim Gress
Jim lives in Pennsylvania.

Rhys Hanna
After sailing around the world for 20 years, Rhys now lives in New Zealand.

Wm. Hofferth
Wm. has done commissions for Graceland and The Mark Twain Museum.

Rick Hutcheson
Rick, resident of Grimes, Iowa, has been scrolling for over 15 years.
www.scrollsaws.com

Gary MacKay
Gary lives in Myrtle Beach, S.C., and enjoys gardening and golf.

Paul Meisel
Paul resides in Mound, Minn., where he is an avid woodworker and designer.

Sue Mey
Sue lives in Pretoria, South Africa.
www.scrollsawartist.com

Stephen Miklos
Stephen teaches scrollsawing and lutherie and the Woodworker's Club in Norwalk, Conn. Visit his website at *www.carrotcreek.com*.

Neal Moore
Neal retired from the Navy to Cottageville, W. Va. in 2002.

John A. Nelson
John, a prolific scroller and designer, contributes frequently to *Scroll Saw Woodworking & Crafts.*
www.scrollsawer.com

Judy and Dave Peterson
Judy and Dave live in Wisconsin. Judy makes the puzzles and Dave runs the business side. They've published several puzzle books with Fox Chapel Publishing.

Richard Preator
Richard, of Peculiar, Mo., owns Peculiar Fretworks, a business dedicated to restoring historic scroll saw patterns.

Judy Gale Roberts and Jerry Booher
Judy and Jerry are known for their intarsia work.
www.intarsia.com.

Jim Stirling
Australian-born Jim is known for using his unique relief techniques to scroll collapsible castles. He lives in Norway.
www.stirling.no

Diana Thompson
Diana, who lives in Theodore, Ala., is a prolific scroller and designer.
www.scrollsawinspirations.com

Kathy Wise
Kathy is known for her intarsia work. She lives in Yale, Mich.
www.kathywise.com

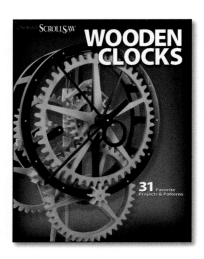
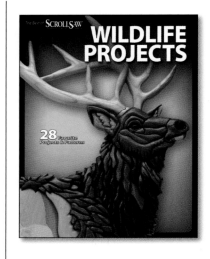
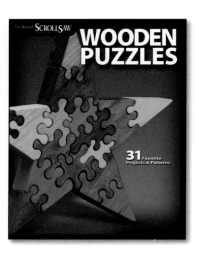
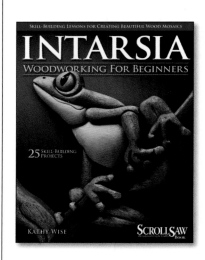
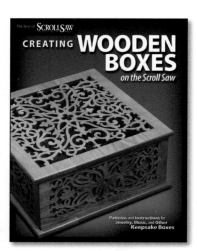
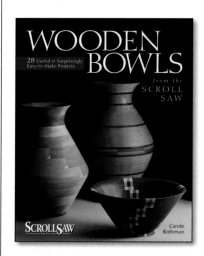

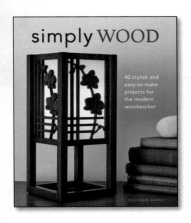

Simply Wood
40 Stylish & Easy To Make Projects for the Modern Woodworker
By Roshaan Ganief

Breathe new life into your scroll saw projects with unique, modern designs that will add beauty and flair to your home decor.

ISBN: 978-1-56523-440-6
$19.95 • 200 Pages

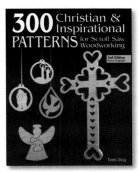

300 Christian and Inspirational Patterns for Scroll Saw Woodworking,
2nd Edition Revised & Expanded

ISBN: 978-1-56523-430-7
$19.95 • 216 Pages

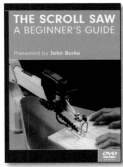

The Scroll Saw: A Beginner's Guide–DVD

ISBN: 978-1-56523-411-6
$19.95 • 65 Minutes

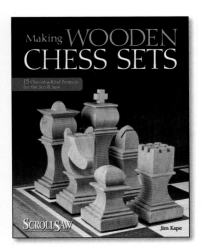

Making Wooden Chess Sets
15 One-of-a Kind Designs for the Scroll Saw
By Jim Kape

Unique, heirloom quality chess set designs that will inspire collectors, players, scrollers and woodworkers to craft and display their beautiful works of art.

ISBN: 978-1-56523-457-4
$19.95 • 136 Pages

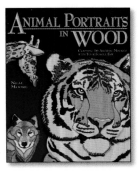

Animal Portraits in Wood

ISBN: 978-1-56523-293-8
$17.95 • 128 Pages

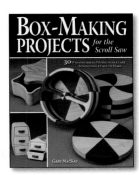

Box-Making Projects for the Scroll Saw

ISBN: 978-1-56523-294-5
$17.95 • 144 Pages

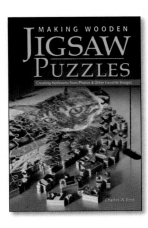

Making Wooden Jigsaw Puzzles
Creating Heirlooms from Photos & Other Favorite Images
By Charles W. Ross

Tips and tricks for both beginner and experienced scroll saw woodworkers to make personalized and challenging puzzles from photos and digital images.

ISBN 978-1-56523-480-2
$14.95 • 104 Pages

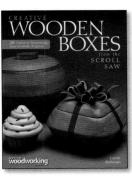

Creative Wooden Boxes from the Scroll Saw
28 Useful & Surprisingly Easy-to-Make Projects

ISBN: 978-1-56523-541-0
$24.95 • 176 Pages

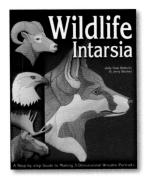

Wildlife Intarsia
A Step-by-Step Guide to Making 3-Dimensional Wooden Portraits

ISBN: 978-1-56523-282-2
$19.95 • 128 Pages

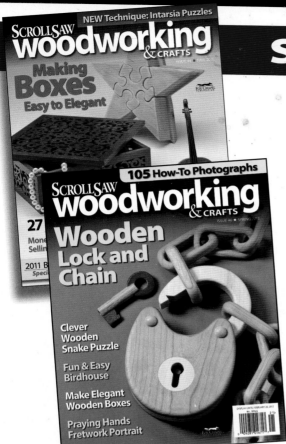